"*From This Day Forward*, a love story of hope, faith, and forgiveness, is Amy and Matt Baumgardner's incredible story of recovery. It's a frank and honest look at 'everyday alcoholism.' Every town has a Matt and Amy. Their situation is not unique but their recovery is. It's the incredibly inspirational story of a family pulling together in order to recover. I can't recommend it enough."

Veronica Valli, addictions therapist,
author, *Why You Drink and How to Stop*
(in recovery for more than fourteen years)

"Matt and Amy Baumgardner beat the odds and have written a book that shares their experience, strength, and hope in a manner that is both candid and hopeful; more than two decades of work with families in addiction helped me place a high value on those qualities. I look forward to hearing more from this couple on their journey of healing and hope."

Andrea Patten, author,
What Kids Need to Succeed:
Four Foundations of Adult Achievement

"As a child of a deceased alcoholic, I found *From This Day Forward* to be a moving transparent account of how alcohol addiction can ravage a life yet it also shows the transformational power of a life in recovery. For anyone who is struggling with the darkness of addiction . . . this book will show you the light!"

DeVon Franklin, author,
Produced by Faith

from THIS DAY *forward*

A Love Story of Faith, Hope, and Forgiveness

Amy & Matt Baumgardner

with Cynthia DiTiberio

Health Communications, Inc.
Deerfield Beach, Florida

www.hcibooks.com

Names have been changed to protect the privacy of certain individuals.

**Library of Congress Cataloging-in-Publication Data
is available through the Library of Congress.**

© 2014 Amy and Matt Baumgardner

ISBN-13: 978-0-7573-1805-4 (Paperback)
ISBN-10: 0-7573-1805-3 (Paperback)
ISBN-13: 978-0-7573-1806-1 (ePub)
ISBN-10: 0-7573-1806-1 (ePub)

Publisher: Health Communications, Inc.
    3201 S.W. 15th Street
    Deerfield Beach, FL 33442–8190

Cover design by Larissa Hise Henoch
Interior design and formatting by Lawna Patterson Oldfield

To our children,

Gavin, Madison, and Hadley

Contents

PART FOUR: *The Real Rock Bottom*

PART FIVE: *Recovery*

PART SIX: *Reconciliation*

Prologue

Amy

I open my eyes and there is no noise. The windshield in front of me is cracked. A large trail of split glass travels across its plane. I'm rapt in the trace and my eyes follow the splintered glass out to the ends. There is no movement, no noise. All is silent and calm.

Through the windshield, I see a throbbing white light and flashing red colors. I lean forward and squint through the fractured glass, but I can't make anything out. My heart starts to pound like a fist against my chest, and I can feel each thunderous beat.

Everything is moving in slow motion. The sounds around me start to echo through my head and I want to scream. "What is happening?" I yell, but there is no answer.

This is where it all began. On a cold January day with fresh fallen snow on the roads, beautifully formed icicles on tree limbs, and a hopeless drunk behind the wheel of a car. This is where my story ended and a new journey began. Right then, in that moment, on the side of the road, in that accident, was when everything changed for me.

"Oh God, help me!" I cry as I look over and see her. My daughter, cold, hurt, and lying on the dirty ground. The paramedics are frantic around her, and I can feel her fear. She is calling for me but I can't reach her. I can't hold her or comfort her. I hear her sweet voice and I scream out her name. The reality of what I've done hits me. I remember now . . . my children were in the backseat. Oh God, help me, what have I done?

Introduction

Amy

I did a very bad thing. An unforgiveable thing. A thing that destines you to be a leper, someone with an A branded across your chest (though mine could also be a D), a person whom people talk about with disgust and awe and an "aren't you so glad you're not her" tone.

I drove drunk. With my two children in the car.

And we got in an accident.

The details are horrible and scary and shameful. I still cannot believe it happened.

And yet I can. Because for two years, I was owned. Shackled by alcohol.

So this should be a story of sadness and regret and despair. And it is. But it's also a story of hope. And forgiveness. And second chances.

1

It's a story of miracles.

Because today, four years after that fateful day when I did the ultimate wrong, I have a beautiful life. And I have a passion to tell the world that there is light at the end of even the darkest tunnel. Even if you've messed up in the most epic way, you can move forward.

The fact is, I was a liar, a cheat, a negligent mother, and an abusive wife. The pages that follow are me at my darkest. But I show them to you because I know that it is possible to change; it is possible to remake your life and build a new path that leads someplace entirely . . . magical.

This is our story.

PART ONE
Romance

*It is not a lack of love, but a lack of friendship
that makes unhappy marriages.*

—Friedrich Nietzsche

CHAPTER 1 *Matt*

As I pulled into the driveway, I dreaded the scene before me. I wracked my brain yet again to see if there was some other errand, anything I could do to delay my return. But I knew, no matter what state Amy was in, my children would run up to me with joy, so happy to see me. So that thought propelled me forward as I turned off the car, opened the door, and dragged myself to the front door.

It wasn't always like this. Amy was my childhood sweetheart, someone I had loved my whole life. I couldn't imagine my life without her. But the person she had become in the last two years was unfamiliar, a total stranger. Our fights had gotten vicious, curse words thrown like grenades, aimed to do the ultimate harm.

How many times had I thought about leaving in the last year? Too many to count. But divorce was unheard of in my family.

And as much as I felt like I was living in hell, the thought of picking up and leaving was just as scary as staying.

Amy was the love of my life. I'd first met her in middle school, on a typical day like any other. I was walking to my school bus, thinking about the upcoming weekend. As I climbed aboard, I headed to my usual spot at the back of the bus. It was where the cool kids sat, the who's who of middle school. Being an eighth grader gave you some privileges, and sitting in the back of the bus was one of them.

But as I strutted to the back row, I came up short. There was a brown-haired girl sitting on my throne.

I looked at my friends in confusion. *Who let this girl take my seat? What was she doing there?* I mean, sure, she was cute, but shouldn't one of them have said something? They looked at me, shrugged their shoulders, and kept their mouths shut.

As the bus lunged forward, there was nothing to do but sit down in the only seat still available, much closer to the middle of the bus than I was comfortable with.

My stop was the first stop, so I knew I didn't have long to question this new girl and explain that, though I was letting her have that seat for now, it wasn't going to be a regular thing. Luckily, as I glanced back at my friend Todd, he took the bait and started questioning her.

What's your name?

Where are you from?

Where do you live?

This was the usual questioning for a new kid. The girl answered each one openly, like she'd been doing this all her life. She was not shy, at least not in the way one would expect from a new girl in an unfamiliar setting. In fact, she commanded respect and made everyone listening feel like there was a new sheriff in town.

Her name was Amy and she'd just moved from Philadelphia. Her mother had kicked her out and she had come to live with her aunt.

I stared. *What had this girl done that was so terrible to get kicked out of her house?* We lived in Oxford, a small town, a place that didn't know scandal, where everyone knew each other, and we could hardly imagine being separated from our families who tethered us to them like dogs on a leash. No one ever got too far.

Someone was brave enough to ask, "Why did she kick you out?"

The girl smirked and looked me directly in the eye. "I'm pregnant," she said proudly.

The bus was silent. My guy friends exchanged shocked looks. Being eighth graders, we all knew how someone got pregnant, but no one we knew was actually having sex!

As the bus approached my stop, I didn't want to get off. I wanted to hear more. *Someone, please ask the question we're dying to know,* I thought, as I gathered my backpack and shifted its heavy weight onto my shoulders. With one last glance back, I started inching toward the front of the bus. Finally, I heard the question: "So, who's the father?"

I turned around and met her eyes, sparkling with intensity.

"He is," she said, pointing at me. My jaw dropped as all eyes turned toward me. Wide-eyed and stunned at her comment, I watched my friends look at me with confusion. Why would I have kept such a secret? But how could I say I'd never even kissed a girl, that I hadn't seen Amy until that afternoon?

I was embarrassed but elated as I sped down the aisle and jumped off the bus. As the bus pulled away, eyes still on me as they stared out the window, I couldn't wait for the next morning, when I could see this girl again and face my friends. How far would the rumor spill before then? I didn't care. I couldn't believe how my life had changed.

Where earlier that day the only thing I had to look forward to was football over the weekend, I suddenly had a reason to rush to school the next morning.

Fast forward eleven years and I find myself standing at the front of a church, in a black tux, waiting for that beautiful, brown-haired, spunky girl to walk down the aisle to marry me.

CHAPTER 2 *Amy*

"*om?*"

I heard my son Gavin's gentle voice at my door. I opened my eyes and stared at the clock. 7:30. The bus would be coming in fifteen minutes.

I slammed my head back to the pillow, hoping to make it all go away. But there it was again, along with a soft knock. "Mom?"

I gathered every ounce of energy I had to get up, go downstairs, and get my son a bowl of cereal. Matt, being a teacher at the middle school, left early in the morning, so I was on duty to get Gavin ready for kindergarten and out to the bus stop in time. As he slurped his Rice Krispies at the kitchen table, I lay back down on the couch. *If I could only shut my eyes for a few more seconds.*

The next thing I knew, Gavin was shaking my arm, saying, "Mommy, Mommy, the bus, the bus!"

I heard the loud groan of the school bus pulling away from our street and sighed. "Don't worry, Gavin, there's no school today," I murmured, trying to make this better and avoid the fact that I blew it.

He paused and looked at me. Even at his age he knew something was off and that he'd seen the school bus outside his window. He looked down at me and softly said, "Come on, Mommy, I have to go to school today."

The fact was, this wasn't the first time he had missed a day of school because I couldn't function.

Matt would kill me if he knew. Being a teacher himself, nothing was more important than an education for our children. But by now, I'd gotten really good at telling lies.

Some people might say that Matt and I were doomed from the start. It's true that when we first met, I told a whopper of a lie. Obviously I wasn't pregnant. But by the time I was in eighth grade, I had attended six different schools. I knew that the best way to assimilate into a new environment was to make people notice you. I'd been the new kid before, and, when you hung back, waiting for people to make friends with you, you always ended up disappointed, feeling like an outcast, a loser. I said it to be sarcastic and make a mockery of the "new kid" mentality everyone seemed to have. No one was expecting that answer, right? I was instantly the likable, new funny girl and not just another new face.

I hadn't gotten kicked out by my mom either. We had moved to Oxford because she'd married her third husband. Larry didn't have kids of his own and didn't hide the fact that it was an adjustment living with my mom and her three kids. My two older brothers moved out as soon as they could. Peace out, good luck, sis. As the youngest, I was soon the only one left. Larry made it clear that he was counting down the days until I was out of his house.

Whether I liked Larry or not, this marriage seemed to stick and finally I was able to put down some roots. After Matt got over the initial shock of our meeting, we became good friends. We played a husband and wife in freshman English and then sat next to each other the next year in Spanish. We were both athletes and would cheer each other on at events. I knew that Matt had a crush on me, and I was flattered, but I never acknowledged it. He was always just Matt. Always up to something and always good for a laugh.

Matt was a popular guy and had his share of girls interested in him. He liked to consider himself a Casanova, and I often cracked up during Spanish class watching Matt flirt with underclassmen, while his girlfriend peered through the glass of the door halfway through the period. I would nudge Matt and laugh. He knew he was busted. There were even times I ran interference for him if I saw him walking toward the classroom with his girlfriend and one of his other "friends" was waiting at the door to say hello to him before class. I'd distract her so there wouldn't be a scene as Matt kissed his girlfriend good-bye. As Matt sauntered past me, we'd high-five each other. I thought it was hysterical. I just didn't see what those girls saw in him.

The guy I was dating at the time occupied all of my attention. Rick was older, out of high school, popular. He drove a BMW, his father had money. He was able to dote on me in a way that satisfied my emotional cravings. I had never had a true father figure in my life, and Rick assumed the secure male role confidently. He knew how to make a girl feel important—he bought me clothes, took me to dinner, wrote me poems. He paid attention to me. I lapped up his devotion like a drug. At home, I was invisible.

My parents had separated right when I was born. Actually, my mom told me that when I was born, my dad never even came to see me in the hospital. She called him to let him know that she had given birth and that she needed a ride home. Instead of coming to bring his new baby girl home from the hospital, he sent his friend to pick us up. My mom was humiliated and refused to leave with his friend. We went home in a cab.

Although my dad was never a true father, I adored him anyway. He was like an apparition that came and went without me ever knowing when I'd see him again. Sometimes he would call and tell me that he was picking me up for the night. I would pack my bag, wait for him on the front step . . . but he wouldn't show. Half of the time he wouldn't even call to say he wasn't coming, he just left me sitting, waiting until it was too late or dark and my mom made me come inside. The times he did show up, there was always a six-pack on the floor of the car at my feet, alcohol on his breath. I didn't know it was the smell of alcohol. It was just the smell of my dad.

My mom remarried for the first time when I was eight. Ron made a good living, but his job required frequent moves, thus my affinity with being the new kid. Life was good for a while. But two and a half years later, Ron left. Just up in the night walked out on us, never to be heard from again. Left his job, the house, the cars, the bills . . . everything. We couldn't afford the house we were living in, so we were forced to move out of the 5,000-square foot, beautiful stone house and into a mobile home. A trailer in a trailer park.

So when Larry showed up three years later and moved us to Oxford, I didn't know how long it would last. But at least he and my mom gave me wide berth, to come and go as I pleased. They didn't seem to care. I think my mom preferred that I be out of the house so she didn't have to listen to my stepfather nagging me about toothpaste in the sink, dishes put away wrong, towels on the floor, the phone ringing. Little things and everything. I tried to be as incognito as I could because I knew if I saw him, I was going to hear it. He never hit me, but, man, was he an asshole. He once told me that I was like the stray cat that nobody wanted but everyone felt sorry for.

Matt and I lost touch when we headed off to college. I fled to Indiana University of Pennsylvania, eager to get out from under Larry's roof but still hoping to maintain ties with Rick.

But after a few months of long-distance dating, he dumped me. I was crushed. Despite the fact that he had been cheating on me throughout our two-year relationship, I depended on him. He had been a stable presence in my life, no matter how destructive. I felt rudderless without Rick, without a supportive and loving home life. What was it with the men in my life, always leaving me?

Then, just as I was starting to put the pieces of my life together, I was coming home drunk from a party when I was sexually assaulted in a back alley 200 yards from my apartment. Wrong place at the wrong time. This did nothing to improve my relationship with men. Add to the fact that this was one of the few times my father contacted me. Not to see how I was doing, but to question the ER charge that showed up on his insurance. I had to explain something incredibly personal and embarrassing and shameful to a guy who only cared about how much the incident was costing him. I had never felt so low.

I couldn't imagine having to face the scene of the rape every time I walked to class, so despite Larry's protestations, I moved back home and started commuting to West Chester University. And I reached out to Rick again. I knew I didn't love him anymore, but there was just something about having him in my life that made it easier to breathe. I needed to feel safe and secure, and Rick provided that. He got me out of the house and away from my thoughts. And I was desperate to feel like I belonged somewhere.

But little did I know that a true refuge was awaiting me in Matt.

• • •

"Amy!"

It was the Wednesday night before Thanksgiving, a guaranteed time to run into high school friends at the local pub. I had just gotten a drink from the bar and was heading back to my circle of friends when I saw Steve, a blond-haired, blue-eyed blast from my past standing in front of me. "Amy!" he yelled again as I approached and we threw our arms around each other in excitement.

"Steve, man, you look good! It's been so long." I said. As I pulled back from our hug, I glanced around him and noticed his friend standing behind him. *Wow*, I thought. *That guy is attractive.*

Steve motioned toward his friend and said: "You remember Matt . . ."

I think my jaw dropped to the floor. Of course I remembered Matt. I just didn't remember him looking this good. In shock at the man standing in front of me, I pictured the boy I knew in school. *How could two years make such a difference?* My face pink over what I'm sure was my obvious approval, I leaned in to give this masterpiece of a man a long squeeze. I fumbled over my words as we had a brief exchange of "how've you been" and "great to see you." My heart was pounding as I headed back to my girlfriends.

As the night progressed, it was hard not to look for Matt each time I walked back to the bar. I made a point to sashay past his table whenever my group needed another round. Our eyes would meet and he'd wink.

The next morning I woke up with a headache and Matt on the brain. I smiled every time I thought of him, which made for a great distraction from my hangover.

I didn't see him again until summer break, everyone back from their respective colleges and eager to drink and party with few responsibilities. We bumped into each other around town several times. Each time I saw him I got butterflies, a feeling I'd never experienced before. But I was still dating Rick, not really looking for anything else.

One summer night Matt invited a few people over to his parents' house to swim. I was excited for the chance to see him again and took special care to pick out my cutest bikini. I knew I wanted him to notice me.

As people mingled in the backyard, and I found a spot in the hot tub, I saw Matt across the pool. Of course his shirt was off, and it was the first time I saw Matt in a . . . well, not as a friend, put it that way. I couldn't believe how hot he was. *Why had I not seen this before?* My eyes followed his every move and I knew then that I was in *trouble*!

A week later, I got a call in the afternoon from one of my best friends. One of our buddies was planning a huge party at an old landfill their family owned. (Yes, Oxford was such a small town that the big party of the summer happened at a landfill). After quickly deciding to pitch a tent to make a night of it, we headed out into the summer dusk.

The crickets were chirping, the beer was free, and I was feeling peaceful and happy for once. By the time Matt made an appearance, I was already drunk. Inhibitions long gone, I called out his name, ran up to him, and threw my arms around his bulky shoulders and wrapped my legs around his waist. As he twirled me around, I felt every muscle he'd built over the years and I didn't want to let go. But I finally did, stumbling to my feet with a laugh. He grabbed my arm to steady me as our eyes met. A tingling, nervous, giddy feeling washed over me. Before I even knew what I was doing, I looked right at him, grabbed his shirt, pulled him close, and stuck my tongue down his throat. There's no other way to say it. It was not a gentle, smooth first kiss. I went in for the kill.

After I pulled away, I smiled at him, he smiled widely back, and I walked away thinking to myself, *I've been waiting since Thanksgiving to do that.*

CHAPTER 3 *Matt*

I had always had a crush on Amy. Let's be honest, I had a crush on all the pretty girls in high school. But despite our friendship, she never expressed any interest in me romantically. I knew she only had eyes for Rick and I had enough attention from other girls.

When I went to college, I continued to play the field. I was a football player and thus part of the "in" crowd. Being an athlete meant there were a lot of women available to me. I hate to say it, but there was always another girl. Once Amy and I reconnected, she started visiting every weekend, so there was no room for other girls; I knew I had it bad. My friends gave me a hard time about it, but I didn't care. I just wanted to spend time with Amy.

I knew Amy's home life was rough, that she never felt comfortable in Larry's house. So eventually she started coming up

Thursday evenings and leaving Monday mornings to get back in time for her midmorning class. I was glad to have her and encouraged her to stay the course and finish college; I told her that before long we'd be able to make a life for ourselves.

I wasn't just giving her sweet talk. By the time graduation rolled around, I knew that I wanted to ask Amy to marry me.

My upbringing had been the opposite of Amy's. With two loving parents, a brother, and a sister, we'd lived in Oxford our whole lives. Both of my parents are staunch Roman Catholics and we come from an extended family where there is no history of divorce. None. They may not have had the happiest of marriages, but they stayed together, as God intends.

So I didn't take marriage lightly. I knew that I wanted Amy to be by my side for the rest of my life. I wanted her to be the mother of my children, and I wanted to provide a safe, secure home for her, something she'd never experienced.

• • •

As Amy will attest, I'm someone who has a bit of an ego, so I wanted our engagement to be a big spectacle. I thought the perfect opportunity might be during the cruise Amy had planned as my graduation present. Not only would we be off in exotic locations, but I knew there would be plenty of romantic occasions to pop the question.

We embarked on our five-day cruise to the Bahamas. I hadn't completely thought things through when I packed Amy's $16,000 uninsured ring in my carry-on, which was placed under the bus on our way to the port. I didn't see the bag again until it was sitting outside our cabin several hours later. That began a nonstop shuffle of where to place the ring where it was safe, but where Amy wouldn't find it. I had a feeling she suspected a proposal on this trip and I didn't want anything to ruin the surprise.

After several nights on the ship, we became fast friends with two couples. I decided to let them in on my secret to see if they might help me come up with the perfect plan.

Every night, we sat down to a lavish dinner in one of the ballrooms. After much discussion over cocktails one night when Amy had already gone to bed, we came up with the idea that a cake would be delivered to our table, full of candles, with the word "Congratulations." Hopefully the entire cruise would watch as it happened and I could both surprise Amy and have the big moment I was dreaming of.

But first, I had some work to do. First of all, I wanted our friends to be seated with us at the table that night, so they could enjoy the moment with us and take pictures. Then I talked to the catering staff about a cake. They were thrilled to be part of the plan and happily accommodated my request.

The night of the proposal, Amy and I both got dressed up for one of the formal dinners, and were both excited for a night of good food and dancing with our friends. The waitstaff planned to bring out the cake after dinner plates were cleared just before dessert. My palms were sweaty in anticipation as the sounds of clinking glass reverberated across the dining room. I knew it could be any minute now. Our friends' eyes were shining with excitement as I kept checking my pocket where the ring was hidden. Amy was oblivious, just enjoying the night, no clue that something was afoot.

Then I saw some waiters begin pushing the cake out from the kitchen and toward our table. Their smiles shone in the glow of the candles they had sprinkled around the perimeter of the cake. I watched Amy's face. At first, she thought I was playing a joke. We often told the servers at restaurants that it was the other's birthday in order to embarrass each other. She looked at me with a twinkle in her eye, about to protest, when she saw what was written on the cake: "Congratulations."

I saw her look at it in confusion. *Shouldn't it say Happy Birthday?* She hadn't noticed me get up, walk to the center of the dance floor, and get down on one knee.

I had to give my compliments to the staff of the cruise. The lights were dimmed and a spotlight was centered on me. Our friends stood up and got their cameras out as Amy turned around and spotted me.

Her face crumpled as she saw me, and she covered her mouth with both hands in total shock. She came running over to me nodding and saying, "Yes! Yes!" before I even had the chance to ask anything. As I gathered her in my arms, I said: "Amy, will you marry me?" She nodded again and burst into tears.

The moment was everything I'd hoped for. I had wanted her to feel like the only woman on the ship at that moment, and the attention we received was just what I wanted. The rest of the trip, other travelers would walk up to us and congratulate us. It made the proposal feel like a weeklong event.

When we returned from the cruise, her mom and aunts and my parents met us at the gate with signs and balloons. It was a true moment of celebration, of hope, of knowing that the future we had together was nothing but bright. Amy was the love of my life and I couldn't wait to see where the years would take us.

CHAPTER 4 *Amy*

My heart stopped when I saw Matt down on one knee. I had searched our cabin up and down looking for a ring. But ultimately, I didn't care. I felt like I'd won the lottery. I couldn't believe that a man this attractive, this together, with a real family life, wanted me to be his wife. Finally, I was in a relationship with someone who loved me back, and I couldn't wait to start our official life together.

We moved in together in the fall after graduation, despite Matt's Catholic parents' reservations. But this wasn't the '50s anymore. Matt and I wanted to take the time to plan a beautiful wedding, but it just didn't make sense to live in two different places and pay two separate rents. We were spending every night together anyway.

We got married the next summer, Matt got a job as a teacher at the local middle school, and I had secured a job as an intervention specialist at the same school. We were living a beautiful, suburban life in our small town, reconnecting with high school friends and making new friends. We had a rule—we never went anywhere without each other. It truly worked for us. Matt and I were best friends. We worked, played, and lived together.

But in a small town, there isn't much to do besides drink. Quickly, our entire social network began to revolve around booze. While both of us drank in college, it wasn't a huge part of our lives, but, in our early twenties, it started to dominate every "fun" activity. Matt joined a softball league and most of our summer evenings were spent at the ball field. It was a perfect, cheap place to drink. People would bring coolers full of booze and line up chairs along the field. Softball in the summer is what people do in Oxford. It is *the* social scene. And with Matt's athleticism and my "life of the party" personality, we soon became the mascots for Oxford's softball society.

Different people at different times would comment on how much we drank, but I never paid much attention to their opinions. I was young and having fun. Finally, I felt like I truly belonged. Matt and I had so much fun together. I wasn't bothered by what other people thought of me. I was 100 percent focused on my relationship with Matt and making it work.

• • •

"I'm pregnant," I said, my eyes twinkling, waiting for Matt's reaction.

His face registered shock and then he jumped to his feet, grabbed me in a big bear hug, and swung me around. I laughed as he quickly put me down and then picked up the phone. I knew exactly who he was calling: his parents. I knew they would be overjoyed to hear about a new grandchild.

Even though it was only a few months after our wedding, we were thrilled. We always knew we wanted kids and had hoped to get started right away. I felt like this was a great sign. Maybe I was going to get my happily ever after, after all. Loving husband? Check. Stable job? Check. Now a baby on the way? Check.

While I began to go into nesting mode, Matt went into planning mode. Despite being twenty-eight, we were living with very few responsibilities other than our jobs and were still renting a small apartment. I knew Matt hoped to get us into our own home before too long. A consummate planner, Matt had been squirreling away money for our retirement since he was twenty-two, even if it made our day-to-day lives a bit harder. He even took on an extra job bartending on Friday nights to bring in more cash.

On August 3, 2002, our Gavin Grant was born, a beautiful, healthy baby boy. The next year, we bought a house and everything truly started to feel picture perfect.

But when Matt started coming home later and later from his Friday night job, it slowly created a wedge between us. He worked at the country club, not too far from our house. We knew the owners, thus they gave Matt the prime night even though he only worked one night a week. I knew we were thankful for the extra cash it brought in, but, as I was at home with the baby, I started to resent Matt getting these nights on his own to hang out with friends and drink.

Then, just a few weeks before Gavin's first birthday, I was putting some dishes into the dishwasher when I started to feel nauseous. I sat down at the kitchen table with a glass of water. We'd been out at the softball fields the night before and I'd had a few beers but nothing to really give me a hangover. Since being pregnant with Gavin and then nursing, I had slowed my drinking considerably. Plus, having to be home by 7:00 each night to put him to bed didn't leave much time to party.

As I slowly sipped my water, I realized that this wasn't just nausea. I was going to be sick. I raced to the bathroom just in time.

While wiping my mouth and slumping to the bathroom floor, the realization hit me. I wasn't hung over. I was pregnant.

This time there was no elation, no joy. I shuddered as I thought about going through another pregnancy. Matt never seemed to want the good times to stop, and being pregnant meant no drinking, no partying, nothing. And I already had reservations about his bartending gig. While I knew deep down that he had taken the job for financial reasons, there was another side of him that saw that night as a chance to live it up and party like the old days. I knew this pregnancy would just push us farther apart.

But when I told him the news, he acted thrilled and swung me around in his jolly Matt way. He just thought about the joy a new baby would bring—he didn't think about how I'd be feeling for the next nine months and that I'd probably put a damper on his Big Man on Campus persona.

• • •

I scraped the last bits of chocolate cake from the plate and glanced up at Matt. He winked as he drank the last dregs of his glass of wine and motioned to the server for the check. We were on a rare date night, just finishing up dinner at one of our favorite restaurants. I was fully sated and ready to head home and go to bed. Being eight months pregnant meant I was ready to pass out around 9:30 each night.

But Matt wanted to swing by the club for a nightcap. Despite the weight of exhaustion, I didn't want to start a fight. I agreed to go for one drink.

As we walked into the club and headed over to the bar, I spotted Kelly, one of the waitresses I'd befriended on the nights I came up to keep Matt company while he worked. I pulled up a barstool next to her and hoisted myself up as Matt greeted some of our friends at the other end of the bar.

After an hour, I tugged at Matt's arm, trying to convince him that it was time to go. It was getting late and I was exhausted, ready to relieve the babysitter and collapse into bed. I'd done my part by agreeing to this outing. Now it was Matt's turn to compromise.

But as I saw the flush in Matt's cheeks, a buzz already upon him, I could see he didn't want the party to end. Before I could stop him, I heard him invite people over to our house. I shook my head behind his back, miming that I was ready to sleep, that I was too tired for company.

But when we got home, I saw headlights pull into our driveway as we paid the babysitter. I recognized Kelly's car.

I looked at Matt in anger. I remembered specifically telling Kelly that I just wanted to go to bed.

"Matt, I'm exhausted," I said, trying not to let the frustration I felt reach my voice. "There's no way I'm having people drinking here until who knows when." Matt sighed and went out to talk to Kelly and she headed home. But when he came back in, I saw that he was pissed.

"Since when did you get so boring?" he snarled at me, slamming the door. "Why can't you be up for anything, like Kelly?" Kelly was married with kids at home, but she always seemed to be up for another bar, another drink. There was a part of me that admired that about her.

He went to the refrigerator and pulled out a beer. "You used to be fun. What the hell happened?" he muttered under his breath.

"I'm pregnant, you asshole!" I yelled at him, storming out of the kitchen. How could he be so insensitive? It's not like I wanted to be carrying a seven-pound baby in my stomach. He was the one who never wanted me to go on birth control after Gavin's birth. And here I was, having to pay the consequences.

For most of our relationship, I felt like it was Matt and Amy against the world. But once we had kids and started to need to cut back on our partying ways, I felt like we weren't on the same page anymore. I felt like we were at odds, on opposite sides. It truly broke my heart.

PART TWO
Reality

*The way to learn whether a person is
trustworthy is to trust him.*

—Ernest Hemingway

CHAPTER 5 *Matt*

"*Yo, Matt! Another beer, man.*"

"Coming up," I shouted over the hubbub of the bar. I hummed to myself as I pulled the tap.

Friday nights were my favorite night of the week. My job at the country club was a lifeline for me. It allowed me to pretend to be the old Matt: single, with no responsibilities, always up for a good time. While I loved Amy, I've always had a big ego; I've always craved the attention that women will give me if I allow them. And unfortunately, while working at the club, I allowed myself to flirt in ways that probably weren't appropriate.

One woman in particular paid me a lot of attention. She had befriended Amy as well over the many times Amy would pull up a seat at the bar, so I didn't think much of it. She would even babysit our kids sometimes and come to our house for barbecues, so I figured that she just liked to flirt, too.

One night right around Christmas, I was wiping down the bar as we prepared to close for the night. Before I knew it, Kelly sidled up to me. "I have a present for you," she murmured with a big smile.

"Oh yeah," I said, turning toward her.

"It's in my car," she said. "I'll give it to you when our shifts are over." I smiled and said that sounded good. I figured maybe she'd baked some cookies to give to Amy. I didn't give it another thought as I closed down the cash register and went to get my coat.

We walked out to her car, the night cold and crisp. She grabbed my arm to keep warm as we walked briskly to her car, our breath billowing in clouds as we laughed and chatted about that night's shift.

When we got to her car, she unlocked it and pulled out a bag from the backseat, handing it to me with a sly grin on her face. I pulled out the tissue paper to find a small plant. I looked at her with questions in my eyes. *What on earth?*

"Don't you know what that is?" she asked.

I shook my head.

"It's a mistletoe," she said, her breath warming my cheek.

As she pulled back and looked me directly in the eye, my stomach twisted in knots. *What was she talking about?* Both of us were married, and, while I enjoyed our flirtation, there was no way I was going to act on anything.

I took a step back and stammered, "Kelly, I'm married. You're married. I don't know what to say. . . ."

Her eyes lost their sparkle, and it looked like she was embarrassed. *How did she think I was going to react?* I tried to think of something to say to play it off, to salvage our friendship and the friendship she shared with my wife. My wife! What on earth would Amy say?

But Kelly pulled back quickly and said it was just a joke. Before I could say anything else, she got into her car and drove away. I stumbled to my car, confused about what had just happened. I looked at the plant I was holding in my hands. *What am I supposed to do with this now?* I tossed it on the passenger seat of my car and, after driving out of the parking lot, threw it out the window far enough away from the club that Kelly wouldn't see the remnants there the next day.

I decided then and there I wouldn't tell Amy. There wasn't anything to tell anyway. Nothing had happened. And maybe Kelly really did mean it as a joke. Plus, if I told Amy, she wouldn't want us working together anymore, and she was already having reservations about my bartending job. I knew she'd probably ask me to quit, and I couldn't imagine finding a better fit for a second job. Plus, I loved my nights "off" working there.

But my ego couldn't resist telling someone. I was at the gym the next day with some buddies when I decided to share the story, maybe even embellishing it a bit. I thought they would think it was funny. They had a good laugh. And that was that. I never told Amy and I didn't think about it again.

That was a big mistake.

CHAPTER 6 *Amy*

I *pulled the cookies out of the oven,* smiling at the aroma that began to fill the kitchen. I was baking Matt's favorite as a surprise when he got home from work. I was home on maternity leave after the birth of our beautiful baby girl, Madison, due to go back to work in just a few more weeks. With two kids, our household was a lot more chaotic, but Matt was such a good father, getting home from school in the afternoons to relieve me so I could go to the gym or have some time to myself. These cookies were a thank-you to him.

I was in a good mood because we'd gotten a babysitter for the night so that I could join him at the club while he worked. I sighed in anticipation of the feeling a night out would give me. Freedom. Fun. Amy, the life of the party, instead of just Amy, the mom.

Later that night, Matt was pouring drinks at the bar, while I cozied up with our group of friends, nursing a second beer, feeling a buzz coming on. I was drinking a bit more than usual. My ex-boyfriend Rick and his fiancée were at the club that night. She had her posse of girlfriends surrounding her like a pack of wolves, and I tried to avoid their section of the bar as much as possible.

It was starting to get late, the club increasingly more crowded as I felt a tap on my shoulder. I spun around to see Ashley, an honorary "wolf-pack" member. We had been good friends at one point but these days I definitely knew where Ashley's loyalty lay—and it wasn't with me. My stomach clenched. Why would she want to be seen with me when Rick and his spectators were watching, like hawks?

But then Ashley pulled me aside, to the corner of the room. She grabbed my hand and whispered in my ear: "I have something to tell you."

The room was darker in the corner, but it was still noisy. She leaned in so that I could hear her. "I just don't want you to be the only one who doesn't know."

She leaned back and her cool blue eyes met mine. There was something in her gaze that made me uneasy. *What was she talking about? Is it Rick? Has he been bad-mouthing me again to his fiancée and friends? What lies is he telling you now?*, I thought. I shook my head, trying to act nonchalant. I sipped my beer. I'm over the drama with Rick. Nothing Ashley says could really shake me.

"Okay . . ." I said, encouraging her to just spit whatever it was out.

Ashley's eyes darted around the room as she pushed a dark brown lock of hair behind her ear. Finally she met my gaze again and cleared her throat.

"Just ask Kelly about giving Matt mistletoe," she said.

"Excuse me?" I asked. *Did I hear her right?*

What is she talking about? I had a number of friends who had commented on Matt and Kelly's seemingly close friendship, but I always defended them. I trusted Matt and knew he would never cheat on me. Kelly was by now a good friend of mine, someone who I confided in, who sometimes babysat for us when we needed a night out. I started to stammer my usual defense of their friendship.

But Ashley wasn't having it. "No, no, seriously; Matt has been bragging that Kelly made a pass at him. He told my husband and the guys at the gym. I just felt like it was time that you knew, too."

I looked around the room, and suddenly felt like everyone was staring at me, like they knew that Ashley had just dropped this bomb and were waiting to see the carnage that ensued. I could feel the tears threatening.

"Kelly is my friend. Matt is my husband," was all I could get out.

Ashley's eyes were filled with sympathy as I rushed past her and out to the patio. I have never worked so hard to hold back tears, but there was no way I was going to give the room the satisfaction of having me break down.

My eyes scanned the patio frantically. I thought I remembered seeing Kelly's husband, Chris, out there earlier tonight. Tears simmered as I registered my panic, and I knew if I didn't get out of there soon, I couldn't hold them back. But my anger trumped all. I saw Chris sitting with a group of people and rushed over. I pulled up a chair and didn't even wait for their conversation to cease.

"Tell your wife she can keep her mistletoe!" I spit out before Chris even knew what was happening. The look on his face told me I wasn't the only one in the dark. I proceeded to tell him what Ashley had told me. I didn't even know what my objective was, but I knew I wasn't going to be alone in my misery. Kelly had crossed the line and I wanted to make sure Chris knew it. I was still in shock and just reacting.

Chris just shook his head calmly and said, "Thanks for telling me." I stormed out of the bar and out to my car. I didn't even want to see Matt. I drove home, packed up my sleeping kids, and drove to my mom's. But the feeling of betrayal followed me there. I couldn't escape it.

• • •

I sat at my mom's kitchen table, a cup of tea growing cold in between my hands. Staring out the window, I watched my mom play with the kids in the backyard. Madison was bundled up in several blankets to keep her warm, but I appreciated the fact that my mom could tell I needed a moment or two alone, without the kids, to calm myself down.

After a fitful night of sleep and countless phone calls from Matt, I woke up feeling like the solid ground that had been supporting me all these years was crumbling. I was slipping and I didn't know what to reach for to keep from falling into the abyss.

But mostly, I had this sick, *Here we go again* feeling in the pit of my stomach. Yet another man had let me down. I thought that with Matt it would be different. But instead, it was just the same. Betrayal. Lies. Leaving.

That morning, I had left the kids at my mom's while I went home to confront Matt. He assured me that nothing had happened between him and Kelly, that he didn't think it was a big deal, which was why he never told me. In fact, the mistletoe incident had happened almost a year ago. A year! So for him it was ancient history. But to me, the sting was so fresh, the betrayal so deep, I couldn't see straight.

"How could you do this, Matt?" I screamed at him. "I've looked like a fool for the last year, and you didn't do anything to prevent that. What happened to Matt and Amy against the world? Is your ego really more important than us being a team?"

Matt shook his head, his eyes filled with remorse. "Amy, I've said I'm sorry a million times. I don't know what else to say. It was stupid of me to tell anyone, and I definitely should have told you. I was dumb. I didn't want you to tell me to quit my job. And I just didn't want to rock the boat."

"Well, now the boat has tipped over!" I yelled, getting up from the table and rushing out the front door, the conversation over before it even really started.

I knew that Matt felt terrible. I saw it in his eyes. But I couldn't get past it. I felt like the fact that my marriage wasn't what it seemed meant that Matt wasn't the solution to the loneliness and unhappiness that had plagued me all my life. It made me feel like I wasn't going to finally be happy, the way I'd felt when I'd walked down the aisle and promised forever with this man.

Even worse, I couldn't believe that after Matt thought Kelly made a pass, he'd allowed her to become a huge part of our lives, my life. Matt let this woman befriend me and watched as I welcomed her into our home and allowed her to watch our children. I had confided in her about mine and Matt's marital problems and my suspicions, and, all the while, he wasn't being honest with me.

He kept this from me because he liked the attention. He bragged to his friends, his friends probably told their wives, the wives told their friends, so soon what was just a guy being a guy sharing a story about some waitress at a bar turned into this massive betrayal that ripped through our relationship like a cancer.

I began to question everything. Was the mistletoe really the only incident? I thought about how many times she had been over to my house. Was he flirting with her at my birthday dinner? Did he ever look at her and wish she had been the one he married? Did he think about her while he was having sex with me? All of these ridiculous thoughts flooded my mind and I couldn't get them to stop.

Nothing Matt said made sense to me anymore. His actions had been so wrong that I refused to see any right in anything.

Soon, with every fight we had, whether it was about bills or who was going to pick up the kids, I would always include a dig about Kelly. I threw this one mistake back in his face over and over and over again.

I didn't know that I was letting all my baggage from the past impact the one relationship that had truly worked for me. All I had known growing up was deceit, distrust, and neglect from the males in my life. My brain and my heart said, *This is how love is supposed to be*—broken and burdened.

When I met Matt and he finally loved me back and came through for me, I put him on a pedestal, I put us on a pedestal. Matt had nowhere to go but down.

But I didn't realize this at the time. Instead, my inability to forgive Matt allowed a destructive pattern to emerge in our marriage. Our trust began to erode. And my self-esteem was destroyed.

CHAPTER 7 *Matt*

I'm not someone who subscribes to the maxim "No regrets."
Sure, I've lived and I've learned, but, more than anything, I
wish I could go back in time and tell Amy about the Kelly
incident, even if it meant me giving up that precious job at the
country club. Was that job worth the demise of our marriage?
But I had no idea how deep this betrayal would affect Amy and
come to infect our entire relationship.

As the kids got older, we started to find equilibrium again.
Sure, Amy would sometimes still deliver Kelly digs, but they
were less frequent. She got a new job, which provided a new
outlet for her energy and enthusiasm. As a community rela-
tions representative for a company that provided services to
doctors' offices, schools, and hospitals, Amy spent a lot of time
on the road, and she enjoyed the freedom of being in a different

place every day rather than chained to a desk. She was named Employee of the Month in December, and I felt like she was finally able to flourish again.

But we'd also started to hang out with a different crowd, a crowd that was of course into drinking, but some of whom were rumored to experiment with . . . well other things. As a middle school teacher, I knew my job was on the line if I was even around the stuff, but Amy liked this new crew and started to stay out later and later. She assured me that they were just out late drinking, but I had my suspicions. I just didn't have any proof unless I was going to attend the parties with her.

But I was starting to lose trust in Amy. As her appearance became more and more haggard after her nights out, I began to question everything she was telling me. Even worse, I started to notice that our credit card bills were getting higher and higher each month. Amy has always been a spender, and, until this new job, she'd never had her own credit card. But given her new responsibilities, she needed to be able to take potential clients out to lunch. She'd then turn the receipts in to her boss and get reimbursed. In theory, those reimbursement checks should have covered the entire balance. But soon, the checks weren't covering her bill.

I started to go over the line-by-line items and I noticed a pattern. There would be two bills for each lunch out. Plus these bills were for $75 to $100, at restaurants like Chili's. I thought back to how Amy always seemed to smell of alcohol when she'd get home at night. I had never questioned her about this. Could she be drinking on her lunch breaks? Could that explain the second bill?

I knew there was no way our salaries could cover $500 a week for alcohol (and that didn't count what we would drink at night at home or on the weekends). I shook my head. I was going to have to confront Amy.

That night, after we put the kids to bed, I knew it was time. I headed downstairs to find Amy sprawled on the couch with a beer in her hand. I grabbed one from the fridge, hoping that if I were drinking, too, she wouldn't suspect that this might be what I knew it truly was—an intervention.

I picked up Amy's feet and placed them in my lap. Maybe this uncommon act of affection would start things off right.

"Whatcha watching?" I asked, looking at the TV. It was a stupid question as I could see that it was *Wheel of Fortune* and that Amy was hardly watching.

"Oh, you know, nothing," she said as she took a swig of her beer then leaned her head back and closed her eyes.

"So, I have to ask you something," I said tentatively, not wanting my frustration to infect the discussion. I knew where we'd end up if I didn't approach this the right way. I didn't want another argument. I just wanted her to stop spending money we didn't have.

"What's up?" she asked, pulling her feet out of my lap and sitting up cross-legged to face me.

I smiled in relief. She wasn't drunk yet. I decided to jump right in.

"Well, I just have some questions about some of the charges on your credit card," I paused, choosing my words carefully. "I know that you use it for lunches with clients, or occasionally for a lunch on your own when you are out on the road, but the company has been pretty good about reimbursing you, right?"

Amy nodded.

I took a sip of my beer, trying to act casual. "Well, lately the balance has been more than your reimbursement checks." Pause. "So I went over some of the bills. . . ." I saw Amy start to stiffen and suspect where this was going. "Sometimes there are two charges per restaurant. I just want to make sure that they aren't double charging you or anything. Do you know why there might be two bills?"

Amy straightened up. *Was she going to come clean or try and come up with some sort of excuse? Here it comes.*

Amy brushed her hair out of her face. "Sometimes clients want to hang out after the official lunch and have some drinks. I know our company wouldn't necessarily expense that, so I put those drinks on another bill. It's not a big deal, but I want to make sure to secure the client, which is good for us in the long run, so I just thought it made sense to keep them happy, even if it costs us a bit of money in the meantime."

Good one, Amy. But could that really explain the daily double charges?

I took a swig of my beer, then nodded my head, trying to seem like I was on her side. "That makes sense. But it seems to be happening every day. I want you to succeed at work, but the charges really start to add up. I'm worried that we'll start losing money each month, even if you get Employee of the Month every month." I knew she was really proud of the accomplishment, but the award didn't come with any financial compensation. I hated to be the numbers guy, but at the end of the day, we didn't want to start going into debt.

"Come on, Matt, that's not going to happen. I'll keep an eye on things and not offer so many drinks next time, okay?" she turned back to the TV, my sign that she wanted this conversation to be over.

I slumped back on the couch, resigned to the fact that this was as far as it was going to go. I didn't feel like she was telling the truth, but I didn't have any proof otherwise. As long as she kept this job, I'd just have to watch her bills like a hawk.

• • •

But I didn't have to watch for long. A few months later, Amy came home and told me she was fired. Her boss started taking another look at those receipts and saw the time stamps on the bills. Even on those days where Amy was on her own for lunch and the bill was $9.95 for a sandwich, she'd be spending four hours at the restaurant. They didn't know about the alcohol bills that were our responsibility, but they quickly realized Amy wasn't being the productive employee they needed.

I truly don't know what happened to Amy after that. It's like the old Amy disappeared and someone else moved into our house in her place. The drinking that had been escalating at nights and on the weekends soon consumed all her waking hours. I would come home from work after a long day teaching and coaching and she would be loaded. At home with our kids, drunk. They'd be parked in front of the TV and Amy would be practically passed out on our bed upstairs. I'd get texts from friends throughout the day that said they'd seen Amy's car parked at our local bar.

I was fed up. Amy was supposed to be at home, looking for work, not wasting her days at the bar. We really needed her income, especially because the credit card she'd had, even though I'd taken it away as soon as she was fired, had a balance of $15,000. Now I was going to have to take more drastic measures to keep her away from access to alcohol. I took away her debit card and gave her ten dollars cash a week for miscellany like gas. How drunk could she get with no money to spend?

I don't know why I neglected the true problem, which was the drinking, and instead looked to tackle the money she had access to. I guess the money was something I could control. The drinking? I had no idea how to address that.

PART THREE
Rock Bottom

*You can't reach what's in front of you until
you let go of what's behind you.*

—Unknown

CHAPTER 8 *Amy*

"*Who did he think he was?*" I muttered under my breath as the garage door slammed, the ten-dollar bill mocking me on the kitchen counter. Another week of prison with only ten dollars to spend, the days stretched endlessly before me. The whole world around me buzzed with other people's interests, careers, deadlines. People with places to go and things to do, but not me. I had nothing to do and nowhere to go.

Once upon a time, I had interests, a career, and things to do. I had a loving husband, a beautiful family, and a thirst for life. Now when I was at home, I hid, sitting alone in my room. I closed myself off to everyone, and Matt closed himself off to me.

Every morning, as soon as I opened my eyes, I felt the depression creeping in. I tried not to allow it to fester within in me, but

I couldn't stop it. It was dark and ugly and heavy. It clouded my mind and fueled my temptations.

My intention at first wasn't to get drunk. My intention was to quiet the inner voice inside my head that was screaming at me to stop screwing up my life. That voice that wouldn't stop pointing out every little thing I was doing wrong. Every thought, every word, every action reminding me of what a mess I was.

The only thing that shut it up was alcohol. The only thing that took my mind off Matt and the cold front that had drifted in between us was booze. But the more I drank, the less likely the sun was to break through the fog that clouded our marriage and our happiness. It was a vicious cycle.

But this latest stunt of his was too much. Taking away my credit card? Leaving me with nothing, not even a debit card, only ten dollars each week to spend on gas? He wasn't my father. He didn't need to treat me like a child.

The truth was, the house was suffocating me. I had to get out, but where can you go if you don't have money to spend? I knew I had to find a way to get my hands on some cash, even if I still didn't have a job. Otherwise, there was no way I was going to survive. I'd already drunk my way through our stash in the house.

As I gulped my now lukewarm beer, finishing the last dregs before throwing the can in the corner of the room, I tried to push past the fogginess in my brain to figure out where Matt and I had cash I could access. He'd blocked my access to our bank accounts. We weren't the kind of family to stash cash under a mattress. Matt was a planner. We had our savings accounts, our checking accounts, our retirement . . . wait. I gripped the kitchen counter, trying to shake the cobwebs out of my brain. Even though I'd been fired, I knew I had a 401(k) at my previous employer. I hadn't done anything with it. It was probably still sitting in an account somewhere. Maybe I could cash that out? Who knew how much was in there, but it had to be enough to get me through at least a few weeks, to buy me a few drinks, get me a few lunches out at the bar with my friends. . . .

After a quick glance in our files, I called the company that held my 401(k), hands shaking in anticipation of the booze or the opportunity to outsmart Matt, I wasn't sure which.

I hung up the phone in shock. Four thousand dollars. Four thousand that they were going to send to me via check, and, if I got to the mail before Matt did, I could put it in a separate bank account and actually have some freedom.

I could almost taste the Jack Daniels at the liquor store down the street. Just a few more days and I'd finally be able to start living again.

I smiled with pride. Well, Matt could try to treat me like a child, but I was smarter than that.

• • •

A few weeks later, I felt like I'd reentered the world. Matt had no way of knowing about the bottles I had stashed in the back of my closet and the lunchtime bar crawl I was enjoying with my new friends. He would ask me what I did each day and I'd lie, saying I was off looking for jobs.

Now equipped with money again, I had the ability to drink as much as I wanted. But today was different. I'd held off on drinking because I was going to a kickboxing class once Matt got home from work. I'd signed up after watching my waistline continue to expand the longer I was unemployed, and the more I was drinking. I'd never considered the number of calories I was putting into my five-foot-eight-inch frame each day, and since alcohol usually kept me from any kind of exercise, I'd put on about twenty-five pounds since being fired.

I saw the way Matt looked at me. A lifelong athlete, Matt always made time to get to the gym, and I usually joined him in the endeavor. But I felt a heaviness in my limbs with the alcohol that prevented me from finding the motivation to move. And by the time he got home from work, I was usually too buzzed to consider doing anything but drinking more, and eventually passing out.

But I couldn't shake off the memory of his running joke. Anytime I put on weight, he'd laugh and say, "I didn't marry a fat girl." He said it with a smile on his face, but I could already see him noticing the extra weight I was carrying. I couldn't take disappointing him in one more thing, so I went back to a practice that had served me well before. Diet pills had once helped me drop down to 118 pounds. I figured they would help me shed the weight along with a few kickboxing classes.

I was feeling bloated and exceptionally large one day, so I just kept popping in one pill after another, waiting for the magic to happen—as if I would instantly drop a size or two if I ingested enough pills.

The pills helped curb my appetite and made me full of energy. By 6:00 PM, when I headed to my class, I couldn't remember the last morsel of food I'd ingested.

I walked into the house after my workout feeling exhausted. I was sweaty and smelly and beat up. My body was shaky and I could barely inch through the door. Matt passed me on my way in as he left for his workout. We went in shifts because of the kids. But at least this kind of tag-team gym time helped it feel like we were being "us" again.

After checking on the kids playing in the basement downstairs, I sat down in the living room with a bottle of water, trying to relax and hydrate myself. Proud of actually sticking with a workout, I couldn't shake a pull of anxiety deep in my belly and my heart was racing. I laid my head against the back of the recliner, my arms propped up on the side of the chair. The TV was on, and, as I stared at its vibrant glow, I noticed my vision was off.

I sat up, blinked my eyes a couple times, and tried to focus on the screen. But as I looked at the characters, I could see who they were but everything around them was blurry. It almost felt like I was looking at the screen with one eye closed.

I limped to the bathroom to look in the mirror. More black spots and now the right side of my face was blurred and faded. I stood there staring at my reflection in the mirror, switching back and forth to cover both eyes. My left eye, then right, then left, then right. I was beginning to get nervous.

I'm too young to have a stroke, right? I did all the things I seemed to remember you were supposed to do to determine whether you were having a stroke: raised my hands above my head, stated my name to my reflection, tried to speak a full sentence.

"Alright, I can do these things," I murmured to myself, temporarily relieved. I shook my head. I probably just needed to rest.

I went back to the living room, this time gingerly lying down on the couch. By now, a weight was descending on my chest, making it hard to breath.

I got up, grabbed the cordless phone, and dialed my mom's phone number.

She answered on the second ring.

"Something's wrong," I quickly stated, trying to take deep breaths.

"What?" she responded, nervously. "Is it Gavin? Madison?" I could hear the fret in her voice.

"No, no, there's something wrong with me. I don't know what's happening!" I broke down in tears, no longer able to hold it together. I described my symptoms through the tears, glad to put into words all the fears that were raging in my head.

"Well, take a deep breath. When's the last time you ate something?" she asked, forever a mother. But she had a point.

"My blood sugar!" I exclaimed.

"Yes, go get a cookie, an apple, and then see if it helps."

I hung up, laughing at my stupidity. Of course, I needed food. I grabbed a cookie from the pantry and an orange juice from the refrigerator and returned to the living room, hoping that maybe whatever was on TV would help to distract me as I got some calories in my system.

But as I sipped my juice, the room grew cold. My stomach felt like it had a million butterflies swirling around in it. My vision was still obscured and my hands were becoming clammy. I reached for the phone and called my mother again.

She answered immediately.

"I'm still not . . . right," I said, unable to keep the quaver out of my voice. Thank God the kids were in the basement. Why was their mother falling apart?

"Okay, okay. I'll be right there, sweetie. Just try to lie down."

I hung up the phone again and tried to do what she told me. Lie down, relax, and wait. As I lay on the couch, my hands began to shake and I couldn't stop them. I was cold then hot, cold then hot. Sweat was trickling down my back and armpits.

When I heard the front door open, I couldn't even get up off the couch. I felt my mom's cool palm against my now clammy forehead, a touch that took me right back to my childhood. I heard her pick up the phone and call 911.

"Mom . . ." I tried to croak out, but I could barely speak. Something was pushing down on my chest and my head was pounding. Was this a heart attack? Oh God, make this feeling stop!

I heard my mom call Matt and explain what was going on and then, before I knew it, paramedics were bursting through the door. "Mom, go down and be with the kids, I don't want them to . . ." I tried to get out as the paramedics wrapped a blood pressure monitor around my arm and inundated me with questions.

"Don't worry, your neighbor Nancy is on her way over and she'll be here until Matt gets home."

I sighed, so thankful to have my mom in charge, taking care of things.

• • •

I opened my eyes and slowly took in my surroundings. I was on a hospital bed, IVs in my arms and oxygen tubes coming from my nose. I couldn't remember the ride here. But there was my mom, seated in the chair next to my bed, looking at me anxiously.

The sound of the curtain opening broke my trance as a young doctor approached with a chart in his hands.

"Amy?" he asked.

I nodded.

"I need to ask, have you been taking anything today? Any pills, alcohol?"

For once, I was glad that today was a day where I waited to drink. "No! I mean, I guess some diet pills, and a water pill. I have the bottles in my purse." I looked at my mom and she dug through my purse sitting in her lap. She handed two bottles over to the doctor.

He glanced at them, looking at the instruction panel on the back.

"Do you know how many you've taken today?"

I wracked my brain. "Umm, just one of the water pills," I paused. "The diet pills? Maybe three this morning, three this afternoon, and three before my kickboxing class?"

The doctor glanced at me over the rims of his glasses. "You're only supposed to take one pill for each dosage. So one pill, three times a day, not three pills, three times a day. There's a lot of caffeine in these pills. Did you ever at any point feel shaky or overcaffeinated throughout the day?"

I paused. Feeling shaky was a familiar feeling to me. I got it whenever I felt like I needed a drink, so maybe I'd stopped even noticing it. But I nodded my head.

He handed the bottles back to my mom and made some notes on my chart.

"Well, my guess is the caffeine in those pills led you to get dehydrated. In addition, diet pills can cause anxiety. These pills increase your blood pressure and heart rate, and, given the amount that you've taken today, it's no surprise it led to a panic attack. Just make sure to take the recommended dosage, but, if you feel like an anxiety attack may be coming on, I can prescribe a couple pills to take to help manage that."

I nodded, dumbfounded. Panic? I'd never even considered that was what I was experiencing, but now that he'd given it a name, I recognized it for what it was and grabbed the prescription note with desperation as he handed it over.

More pills to take. But I relished the thought. Pills meant a quick fix, an easy solution, something that didn't take introspection or thought. I could pop pills with the best of them.

So I soon had a new supplement to my daily routine. In addition to my diet and water pills, and my daily intake of alcohol, I soon became a pro at identifying the symptoms of panic. My solution was to pop a Lexapro and grab a drink. I ignored the bright red warnings on the pill bottle stating not to take with alcohol. I thought I'd finally figured out the perfect cocktail to keep me even-keeled, relaxed, and checked out.

Now I was not only able to block out the voice in my head but also to quell any anxiety I felt over Matt's continued frustration at my lack of a job. I created a cocoon around me that protected me from any repercussions or, really, any feelings. In my bubble, I felt safe.

CHAPTER 9 *Matt*

*T*he sun slanted through my windshield as I drove home from work, the windows down, breeze ruffling my hair. This was usually the toughest time of day for me, anticipating the scene at home, but today I hadn't received the usual phone calls or texts from friends who would report Amy's car parked outside the local bar at 11:30 in the morning. That didn't mean she didn't go there, but it prevented me from knowing for sure, having my frustration and anger simmer inside all day at school as I awaited coming home to hear her lies and excuses.

Every morning was the same. Amy would wake up with a new resolve and promise to clean the house, do the laundry, have dinner ready when I got home, and, most important, to go to the library to look for work. We'd never had a computer at home since both of us always had one at work, but now that Amy was unemployed, she had to go to the library to use the Internet and search for jobs.

But instead, throughout the day I'd get reports from friends, or I'd come home and Amy would be passed out upstairs or on the couch, no evidence of any job applications, the house still a mess, and, even worse, with evidence of her drinking all day. Why didn't she care? We were barely scraping by and she promised that she understood, that she wanted another job as badly as I wanted her to get one. We knew going into our marriage that my teacher's salary was hardly going to sustain a household, but Amy had always claimed she wanted to work. She wasn't holding up her end of the bargain, in addition to the fact that she was now turning into a completely different woman than I married—a liar, a slob . . . a drunk.

But the beautiful spring day was allowing me to hope. Each day I thought it might be the one that caused things to turn around. Amy would get a lead on an exciting job, and things could get back to normal.

A few miles from home, my cell phone rang. I looked at the screen. Amy. I thought about ignoring it and just waiting until I got home. I didn't want anything to disturb my tenuous good mood. But I answered.

"Hey," I said, my voice clipped, bracing for what was to come.

"Oh, Matt, you're never going to believe what happened!" I could hear the panic in Amy's voice, its high-pitch timber alerting me to trouble.

What now? I thought to myself.

As Amy's words spilled out over each other like she could hardly get the news out fast enough, I took a few deep breaths.

"I mean, I was leaving the parking lot, and I heard this loud crash. Someone threw a rock through our window! I didn't even see who did it but the passenger window is shattered, there's glass everywhere, you've got to see this!"

"You didn't see who did it? Did anyone else see this happen?" I questioned her but, deep down, I was thinking, *nope, nope, nope.* These are lies. Vandalism? In our neighborhood? And where was she, anyway? I didn't give her any money to spend, but she somehow always made it to Numzees. I didn't know if she just had enough pals there that they paid for her drinks, or how exactly she could afford to get wasted every afternoon, but these days, it seemed she always found a way to alcohol.

"No, I didn't see who it was, and I just drove home, I didn't know what to do." Amy rambled on, her words now obviously slurring into each other.

"Did you call the cops? You need to make a report."

"No."

Another sigh.

"Well, I'm almost home. I'll be there in a second and we can figure this out."

I hung up the phone and turned into our subdivision. *I don't even know why I'm being so rational with her,* I thought. I knew she was lying. I knew that she probably messed up the car while she was driving home drunk from the bar and just doesn't want to have to explain herself.

As I pulled in the driveway, I saw her Jeep. Getting out of my car, I walked over to the passenger side to assess the damage.

Sure enough, the passenger window was shattered. But I also noticed paint scraped off along the entire passenger side, and the passenger side mirror was gone.

My insides churned with anger. What? Did she think I was an idiot? It was obvious to me that she did this herself; she probably ran into a tree or a telephone pole. Someone throwing a rock would never have scratched the car and how would she explain the missing mirror? Had she even noticed that it was gone?

What the . . . ?

Despite my Catholic upbringing, a slew of curse words flew through my mind. I was beyond pissed. I knew if I went in there and accused her of lying, it was just going to be another throw-down fight. You couldn't rationalize with her in this state. It was like talking to a child. She'd just yell and somehow turn this around to me and my failures.

I was tempted to just drive away. Leave her to stew with her story. But I knew then I'd still have to face her at the end of the day.

I entered through the front door, trying to gather my wits about me for how to handle this. I set my keys calmly down on the entryway table and placed my workbag in the closet.

Amy was sitting on the couch, her blond hair disheveled and uncombed. She was a mess and anyone could see that from a mile away. When she saw me she straightened up and started in with her story again. "Did you see it? I mean, I don't even know what happened or who would do such a thing . . ." I let her ramble on.

"Well, we've got to call the police. If we want insurance to pay for the damage, they are going to want to see a police report."

I looked at her, trying to see how far she was willing to take this. I saw hesitation flicker in her eyes, but then she walked over to the phone and picked it up, probably thinking that calling the police would make me believe her. But I knew the truth. There was no question in my mind. But maybe I could get the police to deal with this for me. They'd be able to see as clearly as me that her story didn't hold up.

She hung up the phone. "They are sending someone over. They'll be here in fifteen minutes."

I nodded my head, trying to figure out my plan of action. There was no way I was going to sit here with Amy, waiting for the cops. Just being in the room with her, knowing the depths she was going to in order to protect herself, made me sick. I headed toward the front door. "Well, I'm going to go look at the car again."

But as I walked through the foyer, I grabbed my keys. I knew where Amy drank each day and the route she always took home. If I could find evidence of the accident, I could tell the police exactly what happened as soon as they arrived. Amy wouldn't even have to know.

Once in my car, I pulled out of the driveway, heading toward Numzees. It's only a mile or so from home, right downtown, and I drove toward it, keeping my eyes peeled on the other side of the road for glitter, the shattered glass from the passenger window alerting me to the scene of the accident.

About halfway to the bar, I saw a telephone pole with glass around it. I made a U-turn and parked on the side of the road. I knew this telephone pole. It sits dangerously close to the side of the road. You have to be careful to avoid it even if you're sober. I got out and examined the debris. I looked on the pole itself and, sure enough, discovered paint the color of our car. And then, the ultimate kicker. About two feet away sat the passenger side mirror to our car.

I laughed to myself, shaking my head. Deep down I knew this was what I'd find, but the fact that it was here, staring me in my face, the proof of my wife's deception, I almost couldn't believe it. I'd always suspected her of lies, but this was the first time I'd gone searching for proof. I wished it made me feel triumphant. Instead, I felt sick.

I got into my car and hurried back home, hoping to get there before the police.

A squad car was just parking as I pulled into the driveway. I rushed over to the officer who emerged, a heavyset man with the solid, no-nonsense disposition of all the cops in our part of town.

"Hello, sir, I'm Matt Baumgardner; my wife is the one who made the call." I stuck out my hand to shake his.

"Nice to meet you." He headed toward our front door, but I tried to stop him.

"Listen, before we go in. I hate to tell you this, but my wife . . . she's lying. She's drunk and hit a telephone pole on her way home from the bar. She just didn't want me to know the truth," I paused. Took a deep breath. "I went out and I can tell you exactly where it happened. Our passenger side mirror is even still sitting there." I paused again. Ran my fingers through my hair. Sure, I was throwing Amy under the bus, but what choice did I have? She had to realize that these lies had consequences.

"I'm sure this is a bit strange for you, but I'm so sick of this. I'm going to leave and you can go in there and hear her story. I'm sure you'll see the holes. Whatever the consequences for her, I want her to face them. I just can't take this anymore. She's got to realize that she's taking this too far."

The officer shifted his feet, nodded his head slowly. I tried not to be embarrassed. I was sure he saw all kinds of things in his line of work.

"No problem, sir. I'll go inside and question your wife, see what she says, and we'll go from there. Thanks for your honesty." He shook my hand and headed to the front door.

I shuffled back to my car and picked up my cell phone, determined to find a friend to hang with or to just go to the gym. I didn't want to be involved in this kind of deception and figured I would just wait it out, stay away until Amy passed out. Lord knows, these days it never took long.

• • •

I had hoped that my refusing to accept Amy's lies would wake her up to how far she'd fallen. That she would come to me with her tail between her legs and we'd have a heart-to-heart about what we could do to get her back on track.

But that didn't happen. When Amy was charged with filing a false police report, I refused to help her with her legal fees. So she called her dad, who had recently re-entered her life, to help her hire a lawyer and deal with the repercussions. Rather than apologize to me, a few weeks went by and she found a job. It wasn't ideal, a Sunday night bartending gig at a local restaurant, The Brown Derby, but, with tips, it would bring home some extra cash. The Brown Derby was a nice family restaurant; the bar was open only until 10:00, so I figured at least it could help us out temporarily. It seemed to be one step in the right direction, and I thought maybe this was how Amy was making amends.

But doubts began to creep in when each week Amy got home from her shift later and later. The first time it was 10, then 11, and one night, it was midnight, and she still wasn't home. I had called her cell and she promised she was on her way home. But as of 12:30, still no Amy.

As I flipped to SportsCenter again, trying to kill time, I called her one more time and, this time, her phone went straight to voice mail. The familiar anger bubbled up in my stomach. It was a school day the next day and I had to be up early, as usual.

Should I just go to sleep and hope she'll get home eventually? But given her drinking, there was always a part of me that worried that she had drank too much at work and it wasn't safe for her to drive. *Lord knows she's not one to know that it's unwise to get behind the wheel.* We had enough proof of that.

At 1:00 AM, I called once again. This time a man's voice answered.

My stomach dropped. "Is Amy there?" I asked. "It's her husband." I was perched on the edge of the couch, ready to sprint into action if this was a cop or a nurse or someone at the hospital.

I heard some shuffling and muffled voices, and the man came back on the line. "Oh, sorry, man, yeah, she's here but, you know what, I'm taking care of her. She says she'll be home in the morning."

Who was this guy? And where were they? The sketchiness of the whole situation turned my anxiety into anger. "Well, remind her I have to leave for school at seven so I need her home by then," I spat out.

"Sure, man, she says she'll be there."

I hung up, now too angry and shocked to sleep. The past few months Amy had become unrecognizable, the drinking completely subsuming her normal personality. But she'd never not come home.

I stormed up the stairs and tried to get ready for bed. I lay my head down on my pillow, trying to allow sleep to come, but I couldn't help picturing Amy, drunk, with some man I'd never met. I knew there was nothing I could do right now, unless I wanted to wake up the kids and go looking for her, but my anger at her actions only made me want to distance myself from her. *Good, let her stay away; it's probably best for all of us.*

· · ·

The next morning, as my alarm chimed its daily blast, I could see Amy's side of the bed was still empty. I stumbled downstairs to make coffee, hoping I'd see her passed out on the couch, but that was empty, too.

I checked in the garage. Amy's car was still gone.

The anger returned, as I stomped into the kitchen, preparing a pot of coffee. I had an hour before I had to leave for school. *I'll have to call a sub,* I thought. *I'm going to have to wake up the kids, pack them into the car, and go looking for their mother.*

I refused to let my kids see my frustration or despair. Once I'd woken them up and gotten them dressed and fed, I tried to explain that we were going on a treasure hunt and that their mom was the prize. Their wide eyes betrayed their confusion but they went along, probably glad not to be carted off to school as usual. I hoped they were oblivious to the anxiety that was gnawing its way into my heart.

As I pulled out of the driveway, I realized I hadn't even thought about where to start. While Amy sometimes went to her brother's house to drink, I would've recognized his voice on the phone. So I thought I had to head to the restaurant first. I knew The Brown Derby wasn't open, but I figured someone was probably on the property.

We pulled into the empty parking lot. I thought about leaving Gavin and Madison in the car but didn't know how long this would take. I reluctantly unstrapped them from their car seats, and Gavin and Madison trailed after me as I tried the doors. Locked. I knocked, seeing cleaning women inside. One came to the door.

"Hi, I'm looking for my wife, Amy? She works as a bartender here, was on duty last night?"

"Oh, yeah, Amy was here last night. Not sure when she left, but I don't think she's here now." The woman peered over my shoulder at my five- and seven-year-old, probably wondering why they weren't in school.

I was about to turn around, not sure where our next stop would be, when a man walked in through a back doorway. He saw the kids and me and walked over with purpose. "You Amy's family?"

"Yes," I said with a measured voice, trying not to allow my panic to show.

"She's here. Hang on, I'll show you." The old man led us through the main restaurant, out a backdoor, and through an alleyway to a building in the back of the premises.

He took us up a rickety staircase, the stairs creaking and sagging under his weight. I turned around to see my innocent beautiful kids, following along silently. This would be heartbreaking no matter what but the fact that they were with me was killing me.

A row of doorways flanked the balcony, and the man opened the third one down. It was dark inside, dirty, with just a mattress on the floor, trash and clothing heaped in piles all over the floor. There was a lump in the middle of the mattress. The man went over to it, rolled it over, and I saw it was Amy. She was dressed in some old sweats, definitely not the clothes she came to work in last night, and her face was swollen and black and blue. She groaned and rolled back to her stomach. You could smell her from the doorway.

"What the hell happened to her?" I asked, rage threatening to erupt.

The old man shook his head. "She fell down the stairs last night, just plain tumbled head over heels and landed on her face. I think she might have dislocated her shoulder, but I just thought I'd let her sleep it off here."

I turned back around and grabbed the kids by the hand. We stumbled down the steps and I put them in the car.

My heart was pounding. How could I let my kids see that? But what choice did I have? I had to find her.

I picked up my cell and dialed Amy's mom, telling her where we were. She arrived ten minutes later.

"Amy's up there. She's a mess, still wasted, probably has a dislocated shoulder from falling down the stairs. She didn't come home last night, so I had to call a sub and come looking for her this morning." I said all of this matter of fact, not allowing my indignation to come through. But Amy's mom knew. She'd been the recipient of the lies and phone calls as well. She knew how frustrated I was. But Amy's mom always somehow took her side. Always found a way to forgive her actions or find an excuse.

"Listen, I can't deal with this right now. I need to get the kids to school. Take her to the hospital, take her to your house, take her to rehab, I don't care anymore."

I turned back to the car and got in the driver's seat without a backward glance. Now that I'd found her, I didn't want anything to do with Amy. I wished I could return her to her mother for good, to no longer have her in my house or in my heart. I was done, done, done.

The tires squealed as I pulled out of the parking lot, heading toward school. After thirty-five years as a Baumgardner, I knew that marriage was supposed to be for better or worse, but what if the woman you married disappeared and in her place was a stranger? I could deal with Amy disappointing me, but now she wasn't even coming home to her kids. Was this really the life God wanted for me, for *us*, to live?

CHAPTER 10 *Amy*

I woke up with a start. My eyes stung at the light streaming through the window. Where was that coming from? At home, I always kept the curtains closed in my bedroom so that I could sleep as long as I needed to recover from the night before. My eyes squeezed shut as I turned on my side, my head looked to nestle into my down pillow. But this pillow wasn't down, and the pillowcase was rough against my cheek, not like my sheets at home. I slowly opened my eyes again.

Home. I wasn't home. I was in rehab.

The facts came rushing back. The night at the bar, the dislocated shoulder, being in the ER with my mom, hearing the discussion of my drinking float over my head as I lay there in pain. I didn't remember how long I'd been here or what day it was.

I turned onto my back and stared at the ceiling. *Whatever, if being here for a few days gets Mom and Matt off my back, it'll be worth it.* But I didn't have a drinking problem. I wasn't an alcoholic. Depressed, maybe, but not a drunk. All I needed to do was control my drinking better. Be more discreet about what I was drinking and how much I was consuming.

As the days went by, I shut off my mind, cocooning myself in my delusion. This place was beneath me. I didn't belong with these people. I was better than this and I was better than this place. Sitting in a room with a bunch of addicts, it was obvious what was wrong with them and I wasn't one of them. I hadn't stuck a needle in my arm, stolen from anyone, or sold my body. I was only drinking. *Who doesn't need a few drinks at the end of the day to take the edge off?*

The truth was, my drinking was making me miserable, my constant quest for something to quench the thirst inside me unending. Every day, I felt as if I were crawling down a dark and airless tunnel. I was desperate to get to whatever was at the end of that tunnel, only I didn't know what I would find. My arms were being pressed up against my body, making it almost impossible to move, yet I would find a way to get farther and farther down the hole: easing slowly and relentlessly down a long and dim passage, knees scrapping against the hard dirt floor, arms pressed tightly against my rib cage, my shoulders rounded toward my chin and arching my back so with each move I would scrape the top of the tunnel wall leaving me bloody and wounded. That is exactly what an addict will go through if they know a drink or a drug is at the other end. The irony is that I wouldn't stay in a place like that rehab to get well, but I would stay in a place like that tunnel for a drink.

After five days, I checked myself out. Matt picked me up, barely able to meet my gaze. On the way home, we stopped for lunch at a bar. He ordered a beer and I sat salivating at its mere presence on the table. Did he order it out of spite, to mock me, or as a test to see if I could handle it? One would hope that a person leaving a drug and alcohol rehab wouldn't go sit on a bar stool for a bite to eat. But I didn't support my sobriety, Matt didn't understand it, and the two of us hadn't a clue how to manage it.

I sat there, craving a sip, white knuckling my way through the entire lunch, savoring every last drop of beer that touched his callous lips. My mouth ached for a sip, my mind narrowly focused on his glass, I could think of nothing else. That was how sick I was. That was how hard his heart had become.

• • •

After a promise that I wouldn't drink as much, and, if I did, only with Matt, I didn't drink for eight days. *Woo-hoo, look at me!* I thought. *See? I don't have a problem. I can handle it.*

The alcohol tasted that much sweeter after its absence. It felt like coming home.

Of course when Matt walked in the door to find me loaded, he erupted in anger. Who could blame him? I couldn't blame him. I knew I wasn't the wife he wanted. But I didn't know how to escape the tunnel that trapped me, lost in the blackness.

As Matt released another barrage of insults and anger, I paused, gathered whatever composure I had left, and threw the only grenade I had left. "I'm taking the kids, I'm leaving, and I want a divorce."

Not waiting for a reaction, I spun on my heel and stormed up the stairs. I had threatened divorce more times that I could count. I'd thrown my wedding ring in his face, said the most hurtful words I could think of, swore I was done. But I'd never involved the kids.

This time I was going to wake Matt up. Ever since my rehab stint, he'd looked at me with disgust. But I knew that Gavin and Madison were everything to him, his whole world. If I threatened to take them, maybe he'd start looking at me again.

I went into the kids' rooms and started packing suitcases, the phone pressed up against my ear as I called my aunt and told her that the kids and I were coming for the weekend. She lived in Virginia and it was Memorial Day weekend. I could just say that we wanted to get out of the house while we had the time off from school.

As I grabbed clothes from various drawers, folding the tiny shorts and tee shirts carefully, trying to calm myself, I knew what I was really doing. I wanted Matt to see that we needed to change our relationship. I wanted him to see that I was drowning. I wanted him to want me again, to love me again. I wanted things to be the way they were before the drinking.

But instead of talking with him and telling him my truth, I told him lies: "I hate you, I don't love you, I want a divorce." If I was threatening divorce, then the conversation wasn't about how much I was drinking, and if we were talking about divorce, then what better excuse to drink.

I was shouting that I wanted a divorce, but in my heart I was saying, *I need help and I need you to be the strong one now.* I was telling him I hated him, but inside I was really saying that to myself. Every harsh word, every dagger thrown, was directed at him but meant for me.

It felt good to yell and scream nasty, vicious words at him, to curse and cry, and release the tension inside me by any means possible, but the problem was that I didn't mean any of it. I had too much pride to look him in the eyes and tell him I needed him now more than ever. I had too much pride to admit that I was in trouble. There was nothing left of me. I wanted to push him away because I thought the pain would go with him.

I longed for a scene out of a movie when the husband rushes to his wife and pleads for her to stay. I kept waiting for Matt to grab me and hug me tight and tell me that everything was going to be okay, and that we were all going to be okay. But he didn't do that. Instead, he called my bluff or was relieved that his nightmare was finally over.

CHAPTER 11 *Matt*

I turned around, checking the back of my hair in the mirror. Looks good. I shifted and straightened my collar for the second time. I was pleased with my outfit. I looked nice, like I was making an effort, but not too dressed up, like I was trying too hard.

I walked downstairs and grabbed my keys. I was headed to a yacht club, about forty-five minutes away. A Saturday night out, on my own.

Amy had left with the kids that afternoon. As she started to pull out of the garage, I walked over to her window, which was halfway down. She stopped the car and looked me in the eye, the first time she'd done so since her threat. But this time, calm conviction reigned in her eyes.

"I mean it, Matt. I'm done. My mom is going to help me with the lawyer's bills and I'm divorcing you."

The anger that had driven our previous argument had drained out of me. I wanted her to go. For this nightmare to be over.

"Fine, go. I'll see you on Monday night."

With a final wave to Gavin and Madison in the backseat, their questioning eyes pleading for answers, I turned around and walked back inside.

This was it. It was over. Now I could officially move on with my life. A life that didn't include Amy and her alcohol.

Her alcohol. The fact was, alcohol was as much a resident in our house as Amy was. I couldn't escape it. Wherever Amy went, the shadow of her drinking went with her. It was her mistress. She was more devoted to alcohol than me.

As I drove to the club, I relished this first day of my life without Amy. I hadn't had this kind of freedom since my sophomore year of college thirteen years ago. It felt good to have endless possibilities in front of me.

I had picked the yacht club because I knew it had a great outdoor bar area with live music. It was Memorial Day weekend, a beautiful day, and I headed straight to the patio as soon as I arrived and waited for a seat to open up at the bar.

I sipped my beer as I waited, swaying to the jazz music. I saw two women checking me out at the bar but didn't pay too much attention. I was used to this kind of reaction when I went out. In fact, this was why I was here. To be reminded of who I was, that I was smart and attractive; a catch. If Amy was going to be a drunk, then I'd just find someone else.

Before long, a seat opened up next to the women who had been checking me out. I walked over with confidence. We started talking, and when I mentioned that I was going through a divorce, a phrase that I felt rolling easily off my tongue, they squealed in delight and started whispering. Conference over, they looked at me conspiratorially. They had a friend going through the same thing; they thought she would love to meet me. Could they call her to join us? I smiled and said, "Sure thing." Another woman paying me compliments, giving me attention? It sounded great.

It was something I hadn't gotten from Amy in months.

When Melinda arrived, she was blond, petite, and beautiful. We started chatting and I could tell she found me interesting and attractive as well. We bonded over our dedication to the gym and, when she shared that she worked at a local daycare, I told her I taught sixth grade. She didn't believe me. I laughed. I get that a lot. I don't look like someone who has a degree in elementary education, and so people often scoff when I tell them my profession. Because we were flirting and she implied she didn't believe me, I told her she could look me up on my school district's faculty website. I gave her my e-mail address so she could e-mail me when she realized the truth.

It all seemed like innocent fun: a beautiful woman, some flirting and banter back and forth, an exchange of e-mails.

I was just focused on forgetting my troubles with Amy and trying to feel like Matt again.

When Melinda e-mailed me the following week, we started a flirtatious e-mail exchange. It made me feel good that someone was showing me positive attention. I had missed this type of playful interaction. I used to get it from Amy, which I loved. At this point in my life, it could have been any woman who treated me in the way that I missed being treated. I wasn't infatuated with Melinda. I was infatuated with the feeling of being "alive" again and feeling like someone wanted me and appreciated me.

Amy had come home Monday night, with the kids tired and cranky from the long ride, and she went straight to alcohol. We hadn't discussed her threat. I didn't know whether she'd actually gone to a divorce lawyer or not. All I knew was that our marriage, in all the ways that counted, was already over.

CHAPTER 12 *Amy*

The phone rang in the middle of the afternoon. Matt was at work. I was lying on the couch recovering from a surgical procedure I had just had on my leg. In an episode of karmic justice, I was bitten by a brown recluse spider while in Virginia and needed to have a small piece from my midcalf removed, a permanent reminder of my empty threat, of how low my life had gotten.

"Is Matt there?"

Typically, when someone would call for Matt, I was in the practice of saying, "He doesn't live here." It was childish and mean-spirited but this was what our relationship had evolved into.

But I recognized the voice on the other end of the phone. *How do I know you?*, I was thinking as I drummed my fingers to my lips. Then it hit me. This was the same guy who had called earlier in the week asking for Matt. I remembered that I had gotten a weird feeling about the call because of the nervous tone to the man's voice when he asked for my husband.

"No, he's not. Can I take a message?" I asked.

"Is this his wife?" the man said, catching me off guard.

"Yes . . ." I answered hesitantly. But I knew what was coming next. *No. Don't say it*, I thought. *Please GOD not this*, I said to myself, *Not again*.

"I think your husband is seeing my wife."

• • •

A few nights before, Matt and I had gone to dinner. It was the first time we had seriously talked since my trip to Virginia. Despite my threats, I knew that our children needed both parents, that deep down I still loved Matt. But was he done with me?

Halfway through the night and a few drinks later, the conversation between us turned into one of drunken professions of love. We told each other how we wanted things to work and wanted things back to "the way they used to be." Things were going great. But when we were back at the house having a nightcap, I looked at him and pulled the words out of my gut.

"I know."

Matt tilted his head the way a dog shifts his head to the side when he is trying to understand a command.

"I know," I said again.

"Know what?" he replied.

"Come on, Matt. I know that there is something you are not telling me. I know you are hiding something from me, I can feel it."

I could feel it. Despite the words he was saying, despite how well the night had gone, there was a little voice in the back of my mind screaming . . . *Wait a minute, this isn't right, something is up and be careful.*

When Matt shifted in his chair, preparing his response, my whole body knew that he was about to tell me a lie, so I braced for impact.

"I don't know what you mean," he said sheepishly. He could not look me in the eye. He looked down at the drink sitting on the table in front of him, then put it to his lips to take a swig. He was avoiding me and my emotions. His non-response validated my suspicions.

I'm not sure what I expected him to say or do. I just felt like I had to let him know that I was intuitively aware that he was up to something. There was an unspoken understanding between us. He knew he was up to something, and now he was aware that I knew that he was up to something.

So a few days later when I received this phone call, I already knew what it was about. In many ways, I had been expecting it.

Though I had a million questions for this caller—What is your name? How do you know this? Who is your wife?—when I opened my mouth to speak, all that came out was: "I know."

I tried to focus on what the caller was saying. Something about e-mails.

"E-mails. What e-mails?" I had Matt's password to his e-mail account and, believe me, I checked it. I never saw any e-mails between him and this now, other woman. What was he talking about?

"Well, what do they say?"

He went on to read some of the sultry and flirtatious messages between my husband and his wife. I heard him speaking, but I was really trying to assess the damage in my mind and figure out a way to make this appear less than it actually was. Then I heard him read a comment that Matt had written to his wife. A phrase that meant there was no denying that this was really happening and that my husband was really having an affair.

"Tell me something nice," he read.

I wanted to cry. Every couple has a little saying or nicknames or songs for each other. Something they call their own. Matt and I would say that to each other. "Tell me something nice." That was our thing . . . at least it was to me.

In college, before we could get the courage to say, "I love you," we would say, "Tell me something nice." I remembered all of those tender moments we shared with each other, all of the times I wanted to tell him "I love you" but said, "Tell me something nice" instead. All of the times I had playfully said those very words and secretly hoped that this would be the time he answered with "I love you." To me, *Tell me something nice* was more than just words. To me, those words represented us. They were the beginning of something great and pure and honest in my life. Those words symbolized a time in my life when I was falling in love and it was exciting to be alive and the possibilities seemed endless. I had Matt by my side and that was all I needed.

To have him share those words with another woman? It felt like Matt had taken a piece of me and thrown it to the ground and let this other woman walk all over it. *Not only is he cheating on me but now he is saying things to this woman that he would say to me. That was ours.* I expected flirting; I was prepared for that. But when her husband read out loud the phrase *Tell me something nice* I lost it. That sentence was validation that my life was out of control. I couldn't pretend that my marriage was ever going to be the same again, and it was in that one little phrase that the truth came into the light.

I slammed the phone down. I didn't have any other questions. The questions that remained were for Matt. *How could he?* The anger crackled inside and I quickly called Matt's school. Waiting for him to get on the line, the vicious words I wanted to spill were bubbling to the surface, about to boil over. But as soon as he answered, all I could spit out was, "Who is Melinda?"

Silence. I could feel him trying to come up with something on the other end of the phone. "A friend . . ." he said, slowly. I was about to call his bluff when he quickly brushed me off. "We'll talk about it when I get home," he said and hung up the phone.

Oh no he didn't. I called the school back, demanding that they get him again. They probably thought it was an emergency with our kids. I didn't care. When Matt got on the phone again all I could do was scream, "How could you, how could you, how could you?" He hung up again.

There was nowhere else to turn. I turned to the only one I knew would always be there: alcohol.

CHAPTER 13 *Matt*

I slammed my hand against my desk. *Stupid, stupid, stupid.* Nothing had happened with Melinda. Sure, the e-mails had gotten a bit racy on her end. But I felt like Amy's and my marriage was over. A little shameless flirting over e-mail wasn't going to make anything worse between Amy and me. We were already at as low a point as I thought it could go. Rock bottom, if you will.

But I knew Amy wouldn't hear it. I'd let her down again, and she would again use it as an excuse to drink. I just wish I could have prevented her from finding out. We didn't need something else adding fuel to our raging fire.

It was a few short days from summer vacation with the kids and, by the way it was looking to start, I wished I could hide out in school. Although in my mind, the situation with Melinda could have been much worse, I knew this wasn't going to just blow over, not after Kelly.

I was already nervous about what the summer would be like with both of us at home, being confronted all day long with the wreck Amy had become. Usually I can't wait until summer, when I get to become Mr. Mom, spend lots of time at the gym, and plan family vacations. My dad was a teacher as well and I still hold amazing memories of our summers with Daddy-daycare. I knew from a very young age that I wanted that for my kids as well.

The summer started out like any other. I took the kids swimming at my parents' house every day and kept in touch with my work colleagues. We'd get together for barbecues with our families or for rounds of golf. I'd worked at the school for seven years and some of my fellow teachers and I had become great friends.

In particular, everyone always looked forward to seeing each other at Jack's annual Fourth of July barbecue. It was a huge event with live music, horseshoes, volleyball, and great food and drinks. Jack had worked as a gym teacher at the school even longer than me, and his party was always a who's who of the school from teachers to administrators.

As the Fourth approached, I quickly realized we were double booked. One of my college buddies was having a party as well. I decided we'd go to my college party first and then head to Jack's in time for the fireworks.

A hot and humid day, I couldn't wait to get outside and let the kids run and play with lots of friends to entertain them, and

I would have a chance to kick back with a beer. As I ran down the stairs for the tenth time, finally packing everything we'd need for the day in my truck, I had a niggling thought of how Amy might handle herself today. Two parties in a row, with alcohol at both of them, could spell disaster for her. But I was tired of being her babysitter. I didn't feel like I could force her to stay home, so she was going to have to come along. I'd just have to keep an eye on her.

As we pulled up to Alex's house, I leaned over to Amy as she was unbuckling her seat belt. "Just try to take it easy," I whispered in her ear.

Her head whipped around, her eyes full of disgust. "What do you care?" she spat out and then opened the car door, on her way to the front door before I even had the key out of the ignition.

I sighed. I had hoped to start the day on a better note. But I wasn't surprised. Ever since she'd learned about the e-mails from Melinda, her drinking had gotten even more out of control.

I thought back to the night a few weeks ago.

• • •

It was right after school had let out for the summer and I was feeling exhilarated with the freedom that the summer held for me. As usual, Amy had been drinking that day, so I was anxious to escape from the house. One of my neighbors invited me over to play darts in his garage with some of the other guys from the neighborhood. It was the perfect solution: not too far from home but a chance for me to get away from Amy.

After a couple of hours, I walked back to the house to check on Amy, who had invited her friend Julie over—to drink, no less. The kids were already asleep so I headed back down to Mike's, glad that I could relax now in peace.

It was just after midnight when a car careened down the street at high speed.

"Uh, Matt?" Mike said. "That looked like Amy's car."

I brushed him off, explaining that she had the kids and they were asleep and that she wouldn't leave them alone. But Mike insisted. I sighed and walked back up to the house, positive I would find Amy's Jeep Cherokee in the driveway. But when I got to my house, the driveway was empty. I started to run up to the garage. Empty as well. By now, I was at a sprint. I ran up the stairs to check Gavin and Madison's bedroom. Empty.

I stood in the doorway of their bedroom, both shocked and confused. Where would Amy have gone this time of night, with the kids?

I tried her cell phone. No answer. Again. No answer.

Panic set in as I ran back down to Mike's. I knew there was nothing I could do. I'd had several beers, so I didn't feel okay to drive. I was just going to have to wait until Amy came back. Could she have taken them to her mom's, so that she and Julie could go out drinking? Either way, she was hardly sober when I'd checked on her several hours ago. I couldn't imagine she'd been sober enough to drive, even if it was just the few miles to her mom's house.

Mike tried to comfort me as I paced in his driveway. Every few minutes I tried her cell. Still nothing. I thought about calling her mom, checking to see if that's where Amy had gone. I was just about to call when a car sped into our subdivision, tires screeching, and almost clipped Mike's mailbox. There was no doubt about it this time. It was Amy's Jeep. She made a sharp turn into our driveway and slammed the car into park.

I was running toward the house when I heard the sound of more speeding cars and turned to see two police cars, lights flashing, pull into the subdivision and then our driveway. I arrived at the driveway to find Amy outside the car, barely able to stand she was so wasted. The kids were in the backseat asleep. The cops were talking to Amy.

I barged forward. "Sir, this is my wife. I don't know where she took my kids in this state, but this is not okay. Are you kidding me, Amy?" I spit out, disgust spewing in my stomach.

"Sir, if you can get your kids out of the car and take them upstairs, that would be great."

I understood that the officers probably wanted to arrest Amy and didn't want the kids to witness everything. I unpacked Madison first then Gavin from the car, carrying Madison in my arms as Gavin stumbled alongside me, exhausted and confused. I quickly tucked them into bed and rushed back down to the driveway, expecting to see Amy in handcuffs. Finally, someone to take her away. Finally, someone to wake her up to what a mess she was.

But when I walked back outside, the officers were telling Amy to go inside and sober up. That if they had to come to the house again tonight, they would arrest her.

"Wait, why aren't you arresting her now?" I shouted. I could see Mike at the edge of the driveway with some of my other friends. None of us could believe that they wouldn't at least take her to jail for this. "You can see how drunk she is. That she not only drove but with my kids in the car!" I couldn't keep my voice down; I didn't care if the entire neighborhood heard me.

One of the officers tried to pull me aside as the other one led Amy inside. "I'm sorry, sir, but by the time we got here, your wife was already outside of the car. If we don't actually see her behind the wheel with the key in the ignition, we can't actually arrest her."

"You have got to be kidding me!" I slammed my hand against my forehead. How could this be happening? I was filled with disgust, now not just at Amy but at these lazy police officers. What good were they if they wouldn't take someone like Amy off the streets? I tried to calm myself down, to reason with them. "Listen, sir, this is not the first time. She keeps doing this and somehow you guys keep missing it! Aren't you supposed to be keeping our city safe? This woman is a menace. She could have killed someone, or my kids. Don't you care?" All of my frustration and anger at Amy was now directed toward this officer. I was so tired. So tired of yelling at Amy until I was blue in the face. So tired of hoping that the cops would solve my problem, but instead they kept washing their hands of her. If only I were that lucky.

"Again, sir, I'm sorry but there's really nothing I can do."

"So why are you here? How did you find her if you didn't see her driving?"

I was confused. Who had called the cops if they hadn't seen her speeding and swerving on her way home?

"We got a call from the Yellow Dog. Sounds like your wife was there with a friend drinking when one of the patrons noticed the kids sleeping in the car. The Yellow Dog kicked her out and then called us."

What? Amy went to a bar? With the kids in the backseat?

I didn't know why I was surprised. Where else would Amy go this time of night except to go get more booze? But to pack up the kids and leave them in the car?

• • •

As I slowly walked up to Alex's house, I knew things were out of control. But here I was again, trying to "keep an eye on her." Like I could fix things. Or at least keep them from spiraling to such a dangerous place.

Once inside, the kids ran to the backyard, and I scanned the room. I spotted Amy with what I was pretty sure was a rum and Coke in her hand, her drink of choice. Wow, she wasn't wasting any time. Then I saw her eye a tray of Jell-O shots and start chasing those down.

I knew we were headed for a rough night. But we'd just gotten to my buddy's house. I just wanted a chance to kick back and have fun before Amy ruined things for us.

A few hours later we were off to Jack's party. Amy was acting fine, for once, more of a happy buzz than the sloppy drunk I was used to. I hoped that meant we could actually enjoy this next party. Jack always had an awesome fireworks show at the end of the night, and I really hoped we would be able to stay long enough to see it.

As we pulled up to the party, the sun was just beginning to set and it was that beautiful time of night in the summer, with the crickets singing and fireflies starting to alight. Many of my colleagues were in attendance as were some of the administrators at the school and I was glad for the chance to see everyone, share stories from summer break thus far or talk about the new school year.

I was on the back patio, sipping a beer, when I heard a commotion from inside the house. I heard raised voices and scanned the backyard for Amy, who was nowhere to be found.

Deep down I think I knew that the cause of the scene was Amy. I had just hoped that for once the drama wouldn't have to include me.

I turned to go inside, and as I walked through the sliding glass door, into the family room filled with children and fellow teachers, I saw Amy in the middle of everything. Jack's wife was holding her seven-year-old daughter, who was in tears, while Amy was yelling something hardly decipherable.

I quickly walked up to Amy's side and tried to grab her hand. "What's going on?" I asked Jack's wife.

Her eyes met mine with a mix of pity and sadness. "I'm sorry, Matt, you guys need to leave."

I turned to Amy. "What did you do?" I muttered under my breath.

"Nothing! I swear, I don't know what this bitch is talking about," Amy slurred, taking another slurp from her red plastic cup.

I tried to grab the cup but Amy pulled it away, sloshing brown liquid all over the couch.

As she lurched toward the backyard, she turned around. "You know what, fuck you!" she said, spitting out the words like venom. "I didn't do anything to your daughter; who knows why she's crying."

I couldn't react fast enough. I grabbed Amy by the arm and pulled her toward the front of the house. Seeing one of my friends out of the corner of my eye, I asked him to find Gavin and Madison and bring them out to the car. He nodded and rushed off.

I kept my eyes down as I pushed and pulled Amy out the front door and across the lawn, shoving her into the front seat of my truck. I grabbed Gavin and Madison, thankful they hadn't seen this latest escapade of their mother.

As I got into the driver's seat and started to back out, avoiding the glances of the crowd of people that had gathered on the front lawn, Amy rolled down her window. "Fuck you! Fuck all of you!" she yelled, lifting her red cup, which she was still holding, in salute.

I tried to drive straight as pure rage bubbled up inside me. Amy had embarrassed me many times in the past but this was going too far. These were my colleagues, my bosses! How on earth would I ever show my face at school again? They all knew that I had a wife who liked to drink, but now the bold truth was obvious to all—I was married to an alcoholic.

CHAPTER 14 *Amy*

*I*t wasn't until *I woke up* the next afternoon that I realized what I had done. Hazy on the specifics, I tried to replay the night in my mind. But my head hurt and I needed a drink to deal with this. I grabbed a bottle of red wine from the cabinet and poured myself a large glass. The house was quiet. Matt had probably taken the kids to his parents' to swim, their usual summer afternoon activity. I hunkered down with my drink and strained to remember pieces of the evening. All I could remember was that I had been asked to leave and that the night had ended horribly.

I wanted to apologize and recant my words and atrocious behavior but I couldn't—and the truth was, I wouldn't have even known how to start.

I remembered what Matt had said to set me off. The afternoon was warm, the sun shining. But then, as we were about to go into the first barbecue, Matt leaned over. I thought it was for a kiss. But instead he whispered, "Just try to take it easy." That did it. Matt drank, why wasn't I on his ass about his drinking? I felt like a child being scolded and I resented that. I was a grown woman, and if I wanted to get drunk, then I was going to. That was all it took to fuel my descent.

Lately I'd adopted this "I'll show you" mentality. Every time Matt tried to put a cap on my drinking I became outraged. I would act like a two-year-old throwing a tantrum. *Who was he to tell me to "slow down" and "take it easy," or, my favorite, "haven't you had enough?"* What was enough? I never knew so I kept going until eventually I was passing out on the floor of a friend's house or throwing up on my back deck in the middle of the afternoon.

Knowing how deeply I'd embarrassed Matt, I wondered whether this was truly the end of our marriage. While he'd been frustrated with me before, soon I could see in his eyes that he was fed up, done, that he wanted to kick me to the curb but didn't know how to do it.

Once the school year started, he began sleeping on the couch. At first, I hardly noticed. By the time I went to bed, I would pass out, dead to the world. It wouldn't have mattered whether an elephant climbed into bed with me, I wouldn't have had any clue.

But I started to notice his pillow and a blanket piled on the floor next to the couch when I'd stumble down the stairs in the morning. His side of the bed was neat as a pin. And we never had sex anymore. I wanted to blame it on the fact that he was choosing to sleep on the couch. But I knew it was me.

The weight that had begun to pile on after I lost my job had continued to balloon. By the summer, I had put on about forty extra pounds going from a fit 128 to about 170 and rising. I had stopped exercising altogether, and I hadn't been keeping up with coloring my hair. My roots proved that. I was overweight, unattractive, and miserable. I was not the girl he fell in love with in any sense of the phrase; not mentally, not emotionally, and certainly not physically.

One Saturday afternoon, with football on the TV and Matt on the couch and me on the floor, I was feeling insecure and needed some attention so I started fishing for compliments. Matt's eyes glued to the screen, he barely acknowledged my words. When I wasn't hearing what I wanted to hear from him, I started to pick a fight, my insecurity clawing its way to the surface to be heard. I knew he was holding back his true feelings and what he really wanted to say. I just wanted him to look at me, even if it was with disgust. Or so I thought.

Before I knew it, the argument turned into a discussion of my weight, my drinking, and my being absent in our marriage. That I was "not the girl he had married."

I fumed. I already knew that, he didn't have to say it. I felt it. But when he said those words and then followed them with "and I'm just not attracted to you anymore," my heart stopped.

Wow, I thought . . . *he went there.* And while the words hurt, it was the way he said it, so matter of fact. The tone in his voice was so cold. A fatal blow to whatever was left of my ego. *How could he say those words to me?*

I ran up the stairs, slammed my bedroom door, and threw myself across the bed. Tears of shame rolled down my cheeks. I kept replaying his words in my mind over and over and over again. *I'm just not attracted to you anymore.* I wanted him to come upstairs and tell me that he was sorry and that he didn't mean what he said. I wanted to hear that I was beautiful. But the longer I lay there and waited, the more I cried, and the more I realized that we had reached a place in our relationship where not only was the love we had for each other fading but the respect for one another was gone, too. We were now in a place where we could say anything to each other, no matter how hurtful or painful it was to hear.

The past few months, we had started getting into these really nasty fights with relentless name-calling. Words like "bitch" and "asshole" blew through our house like the wind. My mouth can get me into a lot of trouble and my words can sting. My mouth can take a problem from bad to worse in seconds. I had chosen to disregard my husband and his feelings until eventually, he did the same to me. The fact was that we co-existed in our home. We were no longer a couple.

There I sat in the midst of my destruction. My life had become unmanageable. I had created a life for myself that I hated living.

My days were consumed with lies and booze. I started having to make up new lies to cover up the old ones, and I was exhausted trying to keep all my fabrications straight.

But what really hurt was that when Matt said, "I'm just not attracted to you anymore," he finally put into words the fears that had been festering inside me for months. I was no longer outgoing, fun, and enjoyable to be around. I was combative and intolerant. I was lazy and sloppy. My hair, my clothes, my appearance, my children, my husband . . . all came second to my drinking. I had always made my appearance a priority, but now I couldn't even take care of myself. *Poor me*, I thought.

I went to the closet and pulled out my wedding album. I sat on the floor of our bedroom, the album in my lap, flipping through the photos of what once was. The life that I let slip away. What could have been. Who was this beautiful bride? Was it me? How did this happen? I mourned the loss of my old self. The life Matt and I had so happily created together. The life I desperately wanted back. I wanted so badly to change how I was feeling and how I was living my life, but I couldn't see a way to do it. I had drunk my happiness away and it wasn't coming back.

I could sense that I was on a slippery slope, but I didn't think that I had the strength to pull myself out of it. So I did what every alcoholic does. I drank. I drank because I lacked the courage and the confidence to change my perception of myself.

CHAPTER 15 *Matt*

These days, when I looked at Amy, my mouth filled with bitterness, my heart with regrets. How had it come to this? Yes, I didn't like all the weight she'd put on, but if she was the same Amy she had always been, I could've dealt with the added pounds. It was what those pounds represented: the gallons of alcohol she consumed, her lack of drive to do anything, the weight of laziness and selfishness.

I knew Amy was insecure about her appearance and that it made her drink even more. I knew she still harbored fears about my loyalty after Kelly and Melinda. I didn't blame her for that. But there were times her fears escalated into paranoia.

One summer night I was out on the softball field, the game well under way, the stands packed. Probably a hundred people were gathered at the field, drinking, eating, enjoying the long summer day, the light just waning even though it was well after 7:00 PM.

Playing in the outfield, I was focused on the batter up at the plate when I noticed that the umpire was halting play and someone was storming onto the field. I squinted my eyes. Could it be? Yep, that was Amy. And by the looks of things, she was drunk and angry.

I started to jog toward home plate, trying to nip this in the bud. But it was too late, she was already screaming, flailing her arms around, acting deranged.

"Who is it, Matt? Which one? Huh? Who have you been messing around with behind my back?"

I tried to see who she was pointing at, but all I could see was a group of my friends' daughters. Yes, teenagers—but what? Did she really think I was sleeping with one of them? It wasn't even legal! And besides, what would they want with an old man like me?

I couldn't believe how calm I was. I guess I'd gotten used to this. As I approached her, she ran away, saying she didn't want me to touch her. Fine by me, but there was no way I was going to chase her around the ball field like an idiot.

"Amy, get out of here; you're wasted. I'll be home later, after the game."

She looked at me with disgust.

"I mean it," I said, under my breath, "get lost!"

She spun on her heel and stalked back to her car, slamming the door and squealing out of the parking lot.

I raised my glove in salute to my fellow players and the fans. "Sorry, guys," I said softly as I trudged back out of the outfield, turned around, and tried to encourage the umpire to restart the game.

I was thankful for my ball cap so that people couldn't see my face. Now everyone knew the truth. My colleagues, the community. Everyone knew that Amy Baumgardner was a drunk.

• • •

Her paranoia filtered into the week. She couldn't stop herself. "Amy, stop! Where are you going?"

I followed Amy out into the garage. She had thrown open my car door and was rifling through my workbag, angry words slurring as she muttered to herself.

It was Sunday night, after dinner. Amy was drunk again, and somehow questioning where I had been in the afternoon. She had come down the stairs from her room while I was watching TV on the couch, visibly agitated. She was blabbering about me seeing a woman. What woman? Where would she get this? I knew she was insecure after our fight and because we hadn't slept together in months. But that didn't mean I was getting my "fix" somewhere else. Would I never stop paying for the mistakes of the past?

As Amy started to pull papers out of my bag, I realized I was going to have to intervene. I rushed over and tried to pull her out of the truck, to halt the destruction she was causing.

"Amy! Amy! Those are my students' papers! I need to grade them! Stop! You're ripping them! What are you doing?"

Grabbing her upper arm, I dragged her out of the truck. She tried to get up off the ground.

"I know you've been seeing someone. I know there are probably numbers in here of all your girlfriends. You can't keep it from me anymore!" She turned back to my bag, pulling it from its perch on the passenger seat and lurching under the weight, turning it upside down as everything spilled out.

My anger boiled over. Enough. She can say what she wants to me, but what are these students going to say when their hard work is ripped to shreds?

I reached over again, grabbed the bag, and tried to pull Amy back inside. She staggered out of my grasp, grabbing her arm in pain.

I sighed. I wasn't trying to hurt her. I was trying to contain the mess that she was right now.

Her eyes met mine and in them I saw a new determination form. She spun around and ran back into the house. "I'm calling the cops for assault," she yelled over her shoulder.

I sighed as I picked up my bag and the papers scattered all over the garage, smoothing the wrinkled pages. I bent down to look under my car to make sure nothing had fallen under there.

As I walked back into the kitchen, Amy was picking up the phone.

She had another look in her eyes now: haughtiness. It was like she knew something was coming.

I walked over to her and tried to grab her arm again to reason with her.

More times than I'd like to admit, things would start to get almost physical with us. I never hit her, but she certainly tried to strike me. In her anger, she'd call my parents, telling them that I was hitting her, letting them know what their precious son was doing. I just expected to have to deal with another one of those phone calls.

She pulled out of my grip, spinning away from me, the phone pressed up against her ear. "Hi, yes, officer, my husband has physically beaten me."

What? Was she faking? I tried to grab the phone, to yell over her that she was drunk and didn't know what she was talking about.

But Amy hung up the phone with an evil grin. "The state troopers are on their way."

I grabbed the kitchen counter, my head hanging in frustration. Of course the cops would see she was drunk. I could probably reason with them. But what would she say to them? I felt her desperation and knew that she would go to any lengths to cause me pain.

• • •

As I pulled out of the driveway, I wasn't sure if my solution was the right one. I thought I would leave, allow the police to arrive on their own and assess Amy's state, and then hopefully they would recognize the position I was in.

But ten minutes later, while driving down a country road, trying to clear my head, my cell phone rang. A number I didn't recognize.

"Hello, Matt Baumgardner? This is Officer Jones. I'm at your house right now and we need you to return as soon as you can."

"Sir, you see the state my wife is in. I haven't done anything to her. She's just drunk and angry and trying to hurt me."

"I understand that, sir. You don't need to worry but we do need you to return to the house before we can complete our report."

I sighed and performed a U-turn as I thought of our neighbors, who by now were getting used to cop cars in front of our house.

When I pulled up to my house, I could see the troopers in the foyer. Two cars were parked in our driveway. As I approached the front door, the door opened and the state troopers stepped out onto the porch.

"Are you Matt Baumgardner?" one of them asked.

"I am," I said.

The other reached into his pocket and pulled out a pair of handcuffs.

"Sir, please place your hands behind your back. You're under arrest for domestic violence."

I looked at Amy and saw her expression. The haughtiness was gone. In its place was regret. She turned to see Gavin and Madison staring at the scene in front of them from the staircase.

"But . . ." I didn't even know what to say as I felt the cold metal click around my wrists. How could this be happening? They haven't even asked me what happened! How could Amy drive drunk and escape arrest earlier this summer, and here I am, having done nothing, and I get arrested?

My mind was spinning with the repercussions of this. My job, my kids, my parents.

"Don't worry," I said over my shoulder to Gavin and Madison, "Daddy's going to be fine, this is just a misunderstanding."

Inside, my heart was breaking over what they were seeing.

"Wait!" Amy cried, reaching out to one of the police officers. I couldn't hear what she was saying as I was walked out to the car, but it seemed that she felt this ploy had gone far enough. She didn't actually want me to go to jail.

From the backseat of the squad car, I watched Amy go back in the house. Why had she taken things this far? What must Gavin and Madison be thinking?

• • •

It's Sunday night, I realized as I sat handcuffed outside an office, waiting to see what would happen next. *What if I'm still here in the morning? How will I call to get a sub for my class? What if my colleagues hear about this? Could this put my job in jeopardy?*

I could overhear the officers in the office, shuffling papers, discussing my case. I couldn't hear everything but I knew they were talking about me. I had tried to explain myself to the trooper during the drive to the state barracks. He kept silent the entire time, but I told him about Amy's drinking, her paranoia, that she'd been destroying my stuff in my car and that I'd just tried to pull her out.

But he must have been listening. After about twenty minutes, an older man in a different kind of uniform, clearly a superior, walked up. He looked me in the eye and said, "Did you mean to hurt her?"

"No, sir." I said quietly.

"Well, she had some serious bruises on her arm."

I shook my head. I knew what he was referring to. I'd noticed them myself but Amy had come home with them the day before. She'd been drinking with her brother. Honestly, Amy often came home with scratches and bruises, from bumping into things in her drunken state. I hardly noticed anymore. Of course she tried to blame them on me. But would bruises show up that quickly?

After describing the incident to the cop, he nodded. "I've got a nice truck, too. If my wife was getting into it, hurting it?" he shook his head and chuckled. "I'd pull her ass out, too."

With that joke I knew that I was home free. They weren't going to charge me. But they weren't going to allow me to go home that night either. They wanted us both to cool off. So I called my dad, shame filling my voice as I explained that everything was okay, but I needed a ride home from jail. I asked if I could stay at his house for the night.

New low, I thought as I sat there, waiting for my dad to pick me up. Something had to be done. Not just for me, but for my kids. I refused to let them feel confused and ashamed of the spectacle of their parents one more time.

PART FOUR
The Real Rock Bottom

This I say, therefore, and testify in the Lord that you should no longer walk as the rest of the Gentiles walk, in the futility of their mind, having their understanding darkened, being alienated from the life of God, because of the ignorance that is in them, because of the blindness of their heart.

—Ephesians 4:17, NKJV

CHAPTER 16 *Matt*

*B*ut *I didn't act fast enough.* Even though I thought being arrested and sent to jail was rock bottom, it wasn't. It was about to get even worse. I was about to be faced with the nightmare that I should have seen coming. How could I have been so blind?

It was a late Sunday afternoon. The light was almost gone as I sat at my desk in my classroom, wrapping up some final work on my master's degree before heading home. Amy was with her family and the kids ice-skating, a perfect activity for the winter afternoon.

My phone rang, a number I didn't recognize.

"Hello?" I said, stacking papers, getting ready to pack up and head home for supper.

"Hi, I'm sorry to be calling like this, but I think your wife has been in a car accident." The woman's voice sounded panicked.

"Okay," I said, my head trying to digest what she was saying.

"Does your wife drive a dark green Jeep Cherokee?" she asked.

"Yes," I said, fear starting its slow ascent up my spine.

"I'm really sorry, sir, but there's been an accident. It's on Telegraph Road, just past Gallagher. I've called the paramedics and they're on their way. But it's bad. You better come as quick as you can."

I don't even remember saying good-bye. I grabbed my bags and was in my car, screeching out of the parking lot. I knew where I was headed, and it was a good ten- to fifteen-minute drive from the school. I didn't know how I was going to wait that long to know if my family was okay.

My head was spinning with possible scenarios. It had been snowing the day before—maybe Amy had hit some black ice? There were sometimes deer on the highway on that stretch of road. My mind raced as I ran yellow lights, passed cars, did everything I could to make the miles fly past.

I saw red lights up ahead, traffic stopped due to the accident. I pulled onto the shoulder, not slowing a bit, thankful for my truck and four-wheel-drive as I sped past the backup.

Police officers tried to stop my progress but I blasted past them and over the hill to see the scene splayed out before me.

The field was littered with emergency vehicles, lights glaring, people rushing about. I saw the remains of the Jeep, threw my car into park, and rushed out of the car, slipping and sliding over the snow. Two officers tried to stop me, but I shouted, "That's my family!" and ran past them.

I saw an accident scene where there could have been no possible survivors.

CHAPTER 17 *Amy*

"Don't move," *I heard someone say.* I could feel the dashboard pressed up against my legs. I tried to move but was instantly met with a sharp pain in my right shoulder. "Don't move," they said again, only this time with force and authority. I couldn't feel my right leg. I looked down and saw that it was bleeding.

Where was I? What had happened?

• • •

It was a few weeks after Christmas, a snowy January Sunday. Matt had left for school to finish some grading due the next day. The kids were antsy, eager to get out in the snow and burn off some energy. I wanted to hunker down and drink, try to avoid the memories of the latest fight that Matt and I had gotten into.

But the phone rang. My mom had given the grandchildren ice skates for Christmas and she thought this was the perfect time to try them out. My brother Joe and his two kids would be joining her at the ice rink in Delaware. Could we come, too?

I turned to look at Gavin and Madison; their noses were pressed up against the sliding door, hot breath fogging up the cold glass. I sighed and told my mom that we would pack up and be on the road in twenty minutes.

The yelps of glee from my children should have knocked me out of my self-pity party. But as usual, I was lost in my own misery, hardly able to acknowledge the beauty of two innocent souls in front of me.

As we headed out, bundled up and ready for the twenty-mile drive, I realized that I needed to make a pit stop. While I'd pounded two beers at home before heading out, I knew I needed more to keep me going today, to keep the thoughts of my failing marriage and miserable life at bay. So I stopped at a bar on the way and grabbed a six-pack of Coors Lite, five mini-bottles of Southern Comfort, and a four-pack of Sutter Home White Zinfandel.

A rush of relief filled my body as I climbed back into the car well-stocked. I downed one of the mini bottles, feeling the release flow through me like lava, hot and destructive.

After the long drive, too many *Are we there yet*s for my barely buzzed self to handle, I pulled into the parking lot, spotting my brother Joe unpacking his kids from his Jeep. As soon as I pulled the key out of the ignition, I cracked open a White Zin, drank it down, and opened a Coors Lite. Finally, I was starting to feel good and numb, just how I wanted.

I got the kids into their skates and onto the ice before going to the bathroom to down another mini bottle. I was just drunk enough to manage my thoughts but nowhere near where I wanted to be to get me through the emotional wreckage of my mere existence. I kept looking at my phone to see if Matt had checked in. Nothing.

The more I thought about our argument from the night before, the angrier I became. I kept replaying the fight in my mind. What I said, what he said, what I should have said, what we didn't say. I interpreted his not calling as his not caring, and this fueled my cravings for another drink.

I wasn't thinking of anything or anyone else. I was only thinking of myself and how I was hurting.

I went out to the car twice, to check my phone and pound another beer. After my last trip to the car, I stepped out onto the ice. My balance was off and I was starting to see double. But I thought I was safe. *People will just think I can't skate. They'll never suspect I'm drunk.*

The kids were starting to get tired and dusk was approaching. We packed up for the day, getting ready to head home. I flopped myself behind the wheel and had a moment of pause. *I'm not okay to drive.* But then I looked over at my brother in his Jeep backing out of his parking spot. Just that quick, the moment was gone and I put the keys into the ignition and started the engine.

• • •

I opened my eyes to see flashing lights, blinding me. Sharp pain was scorching my right leg and I closed my eyes, trying to pass out again to escape it.

So many times I had thought about giving in to the urge and letting go of the wheel. I would imagine my car drifting off the side of the road into nothing, into anything. It was tempting but I never allowed myself to entertain the idea for long. Is that what had just happened? Did I give in?

Recollections of my drinking throughout the day were now flashing before me. Had I really been that selfish?

But then a sick feeling came over me. Not pain. Not nausea. Realization. That my kids were in the backseat! I tried to turn my head to see them, but I couldn't. I peered out the window, straining to understand the chaos outside the shattered window.

And then I saw her. My five-year-old daughter. On the ground. Crying for me.

CHAPTER 18 *Matt*

The car was barely recognizable. The entire front end was smashed back to the driver's compartment. The driver's side door was gone and the entire car was bent in the middle. The airbags lay limp with bloodstains. Parts of the car were strewn about the snowy ground.

A paramedic approached. "Are you the father?"

I nodded yes, my eyes filling with tears. *Where were my kids? God, please let them be okay!*

"Your daughter and son are in the ambulance already. We need you to get in and accompany them to the hospital."

"Are they okay?" I tried to keep my voice stable.

The paramedic nodded. "Both kids are conscious. Your son seems to just have minor abrasions. We have more serious concerns about your daughter. We need to get her to the hospital as soon as possible."

He led the way to one of the vehicles. As we walked, I saw Amy lying on a stretcher, being pushed to another ambulance. She was teary, bloody, and just glanced at me. She said nothing. I didn't even have time to go to her; I just hopped into the back of the ambulance and saw both of my kids strapped to stretchers.

I tried to hold it together. My kids needed me to be strong right now. Gavin saw me and cried "Daddy!"

I went to his side and stroked his face. "Hey, bud."

I turned to Madison, who had tears streaming down her face. "I know, baby," I said as I tried to hold her hand. I could tell she was in pain. The paramedics closed the ambulance doors and before I knew what was happening, we were moving.

One of the paramedics was in back with me. I tried to catch his attention. "What do you think is wrong with her?" I asked in a hushed voice.

"Well, sir, we don't know exactly until we get an x-ray but we are concerned about internal bleeding. Don't worry, we're going to Christiana Hospital. They have a great trauma unit and will take very good care of you."

I turned back to my kids. Gavin was quiet, staring up at the ceiling. Madison was still crying, gripping my hand as tight as she could, squeezing it harder with every bump of the ambulance. I couldn't imagine what had happened but didn't want to ask them. *We just need to get to the hospital and everything will start to get better,* I told myself. The minutes crept by slowly as my heart rate accelerated.

• • •

I stood outside the glass window, staring in at Madison. She was sedated now, so at least she wasn't in pain anymore.

She had a stage 4 lacerated liver. They were transferring her to A. I. DuPont Children's Hospital in an hour.

Despite my questions, the doctors were still evading any kind of answer. *Would my baby girl be okay?* I knew that if the bleeding didn't stop, she would need emergency surgery. They didn't want to promise me anything, but I was desperate for a glimmer of hope.

Thank God Gavin was okay. He was being discharged later that night. My parents were going to take him home. They'd arrived at the hospital, along with Amy's mom, just a half hour after we arrived. I must have called them in the car on the way to the scene, though I had no memory of doing so.

The sound of footsteps echoed in the hallway and I heard them stop at my side. I turned around to see a state trooper.

"Mr. Baumgardner?" he asked.

"Yes?" I said.

"I just need to get some information from you. Do you have a moment?"

"Sure," I said. Madison wasn't being transferred for another hour, and all I was doing was standing there staring at her, willing her to be okay. This would help me take my mind off how powerless I was feeling.

He went through a series of questions: Amy's full name, social security number, date of birth. I wondered why they weren't getting this information from her. I hadn't given her much thought.

But then memories of her near misses came flying at me. The time she crashed the car drunk but lied about it to the police, the time she took the kids to a bar and drove home with them drunk in the car. There were so many times something horrible could have happened but we'd been spared. *Could she have been drinking today? No,* I thought. *She was with her family and the kids, ice-skating.* But the scene of the accident flashed before me. I hadn't had time to inquire what had happened. *Could she have been drunk?*

I shook my head. I didn't even want to insinuate this to the officer, but I had to know. If Amy was responsible for what happened today . . . my head couldn't even process it. But I cleared my throat.

"Officer, I feel like I have to ask something." I paused, trying to regain my composure. Now that the thought had entered my mind, I felt a deep pull of recognition. "My wife . . ." I struggled to spit out the reprehensible words, the idea that I was potentially blaming all of this on Amy. "She . . . struggles with alcohol. I don't know exactly what happened today, but I'd like for you to check her blood alcohol level. Just in case." I said.

The officer looked up from his papers and met my gaze.

"Well, sir, I'm sorry to say that that's why I'm here."

My head started to pound.

"When they were pulling your wife from the wreckage, we could already smell the alcohol. And there were bottles in the car as well. So yes, this was an incident of drunk driving."

I felt like I was punched in the gut. I felt this news physically. But the shock quickly turned to anger.

My wife. She did this. She did this to Madison. Madison could die because Amy couldn't get a grip. Couldn't figure her shit out enough to keep from drinking on a fucking Sunday afternoon!

I felt tears welling in my eyes. All I could think was that she had to pay. She had to be punished. This was not okay. I wasn't going to let this slide like all the other times.

I turned to the officer again, composure regained, rage now directed. "You have to lock her up. This is not okay. This is not the first time. Please, please, make sure she pays for what she has done."

The officer nodded, understanding filling his eyes. "Believe me, sir, I will. I was once broadsided by a drunk, was stuck in the hospital for weeks recovering thanks to his sloppy ass. We will not go easy on her."

"Thank you. She has had several incidents over the last two years with the police and I don't know how she does it, but she always seems to weasel her way out of trouble. But this is beyond . . ." The lump in my throat prevented me from finishing my sentence. I didn't even know what I was going to say.

"Don't worry, sir. We'll take care of it. Your wife will not go unpunished."

• • •

Again, I stood at a window to a hospital room. But instead of fear and pity filling my heart, I was filled with rage. On the other side of that door was my wife. My drunk wife. A woman who had just practically killed my kids. Two innocent kids who asked only to be loved and protected and looked after.

I turned the handle of the door and walked in. The trooper was in her room packaging up her blood test results for evidence. I could tell Amy saw me out of the corner of her eye, but she stared at the ceiling. As if she could refuse to acknowledge my presence.

"Do you know what you did?" I began, my voice quiet but laced with blame. "Do you know how Madison is? That she could die? That you did that to her?" I spit out. I still stood feet from her bed. I didn't want to get any closer. I could hardly bear to be in her presence, but I wanted her to hear from me before they shipped her off to jail or rehab. I didn't know which, but I knew she wouldn't be coming home.

"You are a worthless mother, the worst human being," I continued.

Finally Amy muttered slowly, quietly, still not looking at me, "Just go."

Was she serious? That was all she had to say for herself? How could she still not take responsibility? Would nothing wake her up?

In my silence, she said it again, but this time at the top of her lungs: "Just go!" her scream bellowed throughout the room.

I had to get out of there. I couldn't stand the sight of her. I never wanted to see her again.

"I don't even care what happens to you anymore," I said as I walked out of the room. I slammed the door behind me and walked back to Madison's room. *She's dead to me,* I thought. *I can never see her face again.*

CHAPTER 19 *Amy*

I stood outside the door to her room, unsure as to whether I was ready for this. To face how much I had betrayed my family. *How would she look? How would she react when she saw me?*

I had just gotten released from the hospital with two broken ribs and a fractured tibia. My mom and aunt had picked me up after my discharge and had driven me home to gather some clothes. I knew I was on my way to rehab, but first I had to see my girl.

Madison had been transferred to the children's hospital because of the severity of her condition. She was now in the pediatric intensive care unit.

I finally gathered the courage to do it. I placed my hand on the door handle and slowly, quietly, opened the door. I didn't want to wake her if she was sleeping. Lord knows that was probably the best way for her to survive what was happening around her.

Her eyes were closed, her little chest rising and falling with her breath. Monitors and tubes probed from every direction. The steady beat of her fragile heart echoed throughout the room.

I hobbled to her bed, trying not to disturb her. But I couldn't help grabbing her hand, holding that precious hand that had reached for me all her life, knowing that I'd be there for her to steady her. Could she ever trust me again?

She opened her eyes and saw me. A smile lit her face. "Mommy!" she squealed in delight. I stroked her hair, kissed her cheek, savoring her smell, her essence.

"Mommy, snuggle!" she said, pure joy in her eyes. I smiled and awkwardly tried to lie down on the bed next to her. We settled in and spent the next hour being just any other mom and daughter. I just tried to soak up my girl, kissing her forehead while the nurses tended to her.

The minutes went by like a mad dash. It was time to leave, time for me to go get help, time for me to be accountable. I gave her one long last kiss on her forehead, whispering "I love you."

As I walked out the door, I turned to smile. I stood for a moment, taking in all I had done. Madison must have known that I needed the assurance because she grinned and said, "Don't worry, Mommy. I forgive you."

My face crumpled as the tears I'd been working so hard to hold back descended. What did she mean? How did she even understand those were the words I needed? How could a five-year-old hear the cries of her desperate mother's heart?

I could barely walk. I leaned on my mother as we walked out to the car. The sheer magnitude of what I had done felt like a weight I couldn't carry. My heart wasn't prepared for this much calamity—I didn't know if any parent's would be. I was devastated at what I had done, at how I had betrayed my children. How could Madison still smile at me, love me, forgive me? She had no idea of how horrible a mother I was.

As we drove to Bowling Green Rehab Center, where I was to spend the next twenty-one days, my mom tried to explain what to expect for the next few weeks. I would get sober in rehab and await charges. The state police weren't sure exactly what to charge me with. DUI, for sure, reckless driving, yes. If Madison didn't make it, vehicular homicide.

I couldn't compute what she was telling me. "What do you mean, if she doesn't make it?" I screamed. "She has to make it!"

I couldn't imagine that my baby girl . . .

I couldn't even finish the thought. I could only sob and cry out. *Oh God, what have I done?*

• • •

"Hi, my name is Amy, and I'm an alcoholic."

I couldn't believe that I had just said those words. That I was admitting that my drinking was no longer something I could control, something I could manage. That instead it was a disease that had taken over me. That had been afflicting me for the last two years, as much as I wanted to deny it.

While the last time I had gone to rehab I had resisted—"This isn't me," "They have a problem, not me"—today, I knew that I belonged here. It was me I needed to fix. Deep down I realized that the "it" for me was admitting to myself that my life had become unmanageable and that I had a problem. "It" was the drink. "It" was the root of my unhappiness. "It" was the need and burning desire to forget who I was and become someone or something else. Alcohol had tricked me into thinking that I had a handle on my life when, in reality, I was dying, slowly and deliberately.

I knew rehab was the only choice. I mean, look at what I had just done! My daughter could have been dying and it would be because of me. But despite my remorse, despite my embarrassment and shame and guilt, I still didn't know how I was going to do it, to get sober and give up alcohol.

Some people say there is a certain recipe that creates alcoholics. Of course, having a family history of drinking is one ingredient. Check. An unstable home environment growing up. Check. Sexual abuse. Check. But I knew that didn't excuse my behavior. I was quickly realizing that the way in which I had coped with all the difficulty of my childhood was the issue. I would push it under the rug. I could pretend with the best of them that nothing was bothering me. I wanted to live by the notion that if I never talked about what was bothering me and forced a smile on my face, then I could float through life unaffected.

I became consumed with the idea of control. Drinking gave me control over what I wanted to ignore. I could control how I was feeling by taking a drink. If I was in a bad mood, I'd drink to get in a better one, and if I was feeling something from my past, I'd drink to forget it. Alcohol allowed me to compartmentalize my emotions, only dealing with the ones on the surface and the ones I chose to acknowledge. Until one day, I lost control. The alcohol turned on me and now "it" was in control and my addiction was born.

That first Sunday both of my parents came, Sundays being visitation days at Bowling Green. My mom sat quietly while we both listened to my father's explanation of the legal battle I was about to face. He had hired a lawyer to be ready whenever the charges came.

I was thankful for my dad's support. After being absent for much of my life, he had started coming around the last few years. He had received a settlement in a lawsuit and actually had some money to spare. He'd paid for my lawyer's bills after my false police report and would again help out with this. But seeing him sitting in front of me here in rehab, my worst fear was being revealed.

When I was younger, I made a promise to myself. I swore to myself that someday I would live the life I always wanted to live and that I would someday have control over my surroundings. When I was little, I hated where I lived, who I lived with, who was around, who wasn't around—all decisions that had been made for me. The one thing I promised myself growing up was that I was going to be a better parent and my children would have a better life. That's why I let myself fall so hard for Matt. I felt that with him I had the chance to keep this promise to myself.

But as I sat there, listening to my father explain what might happen to me, that I could go to jail, leaving behind my children, I realized my worst fears had become my reality. All of the things I so desperately tried not to be were suddenly the very things I was becoming: an absent parent, an alcoholic, a dimmed light.

As he sat there explaining my fate, all I could think of was my children . . . were they like me? Could this disease, this nightmare be forgiven? Could I be forgiven? I looked at my father and I felt a sadness for him. Was my forgiveness what he had been waiting on? And who was I to hold back forgiveness from my father, when I was in need of it from my children? I needed forgiveness; I needed to know it was possible. As I watched my father speak with sincerity and compassion, I realized, in that moment, that, yes, it was possible to forgive the past.

My life, my childhood, and my relationship with my father all started to make sense to me. My addiction started to make sense to me.

I interrupted him, not even listening to what he was saying.

"Dad," I said, grabbing his hands.

He looked at me in confusion.

"Yes," he said.

I tried to speak over the frog in my throat. I knew this was a pivotal moment. That I was about to give him something that he'd probably been longing for all his life.

"I . . . I forgive you," I said, calmness regained as I put into words a feeling that I had held back from him for thirty years.

I heard my mom burst into tears, but I only stared into my dad's eyes, seeing them well up with emotion as he pulled me into a hug.

I knew this was a step. A step for him. A step for me. But I also knew there was so much more work to be done to rebuild my life.

CHAPTER 20 *Matt*

I *ran the steam cleaner over the* last stretch of carpet in Gavin's room and felt a sense of accomplishment as I looked over my work. All the dirt, sucked away, the carpet left spotless, like new. Unsullied.

I moved on to the first floor, the vacuum heavy, as I plodded down the stairs.

In another hour, I would head to the hospital to go visit Madison. While her bleeding had stopped, which meant she didn't need surgery, she still had to stay in the ICU for two weeks before she would be discharged. But her recovery would continue at home. Bed rest for two months to prevent the chance that she might rupture her liver again, which meant no school. She had to sleep on a couch downstairs to prevent any possible injury going up and down the stairs to her bedroom.

I thought back to the day when the doctors finally announced that she was out of the woods. All I remember feeling was sweet relief. The anguish of the last days were over. Yes, it was going to be a long journey to get her back to my vivacious, energetic five-year-old, but at least she was going to live.

I shuddered at the memory of the dark days when I thought we might actually lose her. And began my cleaning again.

In addition to shouldering all the parenting responsibilities while Amy was in rehab, all I had been doing since coming home from the children's hospital was cleaning. And not just regular cleaning. Deep cleaning. Steaming carpets, washing windows, reorganizing closets, and patching walls.

I guess I was trying to get rid of Amy's presence and prepare for a new life without Amy. For life as a single father. And I wanted a fresh start.

• • •

A few days after the accident, once Madison was out of the woods and settled into the ICU at the children's hospital, I returned to the scene of the accident. I'd finally asked the cops what exactly happened, and, while they had pieced together the incident as best they could, I wanted to see for myself where Amy had almost killed our children. I had been driving past it every day visiting Madison in the hospital, and until today I had always averted my gaze, not ready to face what had happened.

The wind was bitter as I opened my truck door on the side of the highway. The snow was gone, but the tire tracks from the accident were still intact. I followed them from where they veered off the highway, toward the tree that was the actual site of impact.

As I walked toward the tree, I felt shocked. How drunk was she that she could veer off the highway and continue driving twenty yards before striking a huge tree? What must Gavin and Madison been thinking when they realized their mom had driven off the road but wasn't responding? How long were they frozen in fear before they felt the impact?

I knelt down once I reached the tree. I felt the gash where the bark was ripped away by the Jeep careening off it, and I saw the scattered glass that still lingered, pieces too small for highway patrol to clean up.

As I felt the cold ground seep in through my pants, the anger that had been festering in my heart slowly seeped out of me. Sobs that had been held prisoner for days rose to the surface. But it wasn't sadness that consumed me. It was gratitude. I couldn't help but pray. Every tear that slowly descended my cheek was a thank-you. *I could have lost my entire family, right here. In just a brief moment, everything worth living for could have been snatched away. I could have lost everything.* The reality of how close to devastation I was . . . that I was spared. I could only thank God.

CHAPTER 21 *Amy*

*H*ow . . . *how do these people get sober?* I thought as I looked around the circle. *How in the world can I ever do this?* I knew that I had to try to stop drinking because I didn't want to lose my family, and I knew that I wanted to try because this life I was living was utter hell. But I just could not picture my life without alcohol. The images of what I would be missing out on—parties, weddings, afternoon cocktails, our summer beach trips—all swarmed in my head. *What the hell was I going to do then? It's impossible,* I told myself. It felt like the rest of my existence was going to be lifeless.

I shifted in my seat, tried to listen to the person talking. The aluminum chair creaked against the linoleum floor. I looked up. Everyone was staring at me. "Sorry," I murmured and tried to stop fidgeting. Again, I looked at the people surrounding me. People of all ages, races, and income brackets. Rehab was the great leveler. I knew they all felt the same way I did: lost, unloved, unwanted, and disposable. So they turned to drugs or alcohol to hide from their pain. Not every person in that place had started out on the same path, but every single person in that facility had ended up in the same place.

I could see that we all had been suffering, and, instead of looking at the others with disgust or pity, I saw them as comrades. I started to feel as if someone understood what I had been bottling up and avoiding for so long. *Finally,* I thought, *someone gets it.*

About a week after entering rehab, I got the news that Madison was finally out of the woods. She was still in intensive care, but she would make a full recovery.

I immediately stepped outside, claiming to want a cigarette. But really, I wanted to be alone. I wanted the space to process that I had been spared. I wouldn't have to face being the one to kill my daughter.

I hadn't realized how much fear I was holding inside me until I heard that news. For the first time since the accident, I felt I could breathe again. I knew I'd fucked up beyond belief, but at least my baby was going to make it.

I rubbed my shoulders, wished I'd brought a jacket. The air was bracing as I breathed a huge exhale, watching the billow of my breath in front of me.

I turned around, grabbed a cigarette from my pocket, and joined the posse at the picnic table smoking. I sat there, letting the murmur of the conversations wash over me. I took a drag and exhaled. And I realized that I felt at peace.

I paused. It was a feeling I could hardly recognize. It had been years since I had felt anything but turmoil. I felt tears well in my eyes. I couldn't believe that here, in this place, was where I was finally feeling a moment of peace. But of course it was because all the alcohol that I had used to dull the pain, had dulled everything. Prevented me from being in the moment, seeing things as they really were. Finally, rehab had stripped away my defenses. And I was realizing that who I was . . . maybe it wasn't that bad.

Even though my life was in shambles, in that moment, I realized that there was a calmness, a quieting, that was seeping in. Surrounded by misfits and criminals, I felt at ease. Just like me, these people were hurting and could not figure out a way to stop the pain. Just like me, these people had made horrible choices and suffered dramatic consequences. Just like me, these people were grasping at hope.

So I listened. I listened to the pregnant teen talk about her need to escape and get high because her boyfriend beat her, then forced her to have sex with his friends for money. I listened as a man struggled with relapsing after ten years of sobriety because the economy had taken his job, his home, his security, and then his pride. I listened as a single mother of three talked about her back injury and taking pills to get through her twelve-hour workdays just to afford health care. I empathized with the wife who turned to alcohol because she felt alone in her marriage and devastated by an affair. I cried along with the boy who just wanted to fit in because all his life he was told he didn't. I prayed with the man who was ashamed at being in yet another rehab and was hoping that this would be the time he made it, and with the young girl who lost her first true love to suicide and didn't know how to deal with death, so she turned to heroin to ease the ache of loss. I sat with the veteran who was diagnosed with PTSD and learned how alcohol, at first, dulled his pain until eventually it, too, became a source of battle.

I heard all of these people share their stories and heartache with me, a stranger, because they just needed to get it out, to tell someone, anyone, that they were in pain and to feel like someone was listening. We didn't want to be addicts. We didn't want to hurt the people we loved.

These were people, not outcasts or unwanted souls. They were individuals who had made a bad decision or gone down the wrong path. They were just like me.

• • •

The next week, I was coming in from having a cigarette when I saw Matt in the office. Jill, one of the staff members, knew my story and motioned for me to come in. Matt didn't look at me. He wasn't here to visit, he said. He was just dropping off clothes for me before going to school that morning. Jill looked at my face. I knew that the desperation I felt to talk to my husband was painted all over my face. She sighed. "Five minutes," Jill said.

"I could get in trouble for this," she muttered as she closed the door to give us some privacy.

We stood there looking at everything else in the room but each other. I wanted him to throw his arms around me and tell me everything was going to be okay. I wanted to grab him and tell him how sorry I was and that I was a fool to let us go. But we just stood there in silence.

"I don't know what to say," he finally said, staring at his hands. I reached out, but he pulled away. I didn't blame him. I knew I had put him through hell the last two years. But the accident, that was the final straw. How could I have put our babies in danger?

Then I noticed it. He wasn't wearing his ring.

During our fights, I don't know how many times I had taken my ring and threatened him with it. Throwing it in his face like it meant nothing at all. Deliberately keeping it in my drawer instead of on my finger, thinking I'd show him I didn't care. But in all our years together, Matt had never taken his off. "When it comes off, it stays off," he would say, and that day it was off.

"Matt . . ." I started, but then the door swung open, Jill returning, our warden to take me back.

She looked at me and smiled a sad smile. "I'm sorry," she said.

I shook my head. I knew she had already done more than she should have.

Matt muttered a "thanks" to Jill and walked out the door. He still hadn't looked me in the eye.

I followed him out the door. Fighting back tears, I watched as he walked away. I watched as the space between us got bigger and bigger until he was gone. He didn't look back.

• • •

When I saw Larry the next Sunday waiting for me in the visitation room, I was touched that he made the effort despite our rocky past. But my heart wasn't in it. All I could wonder was whether Matt would come. *Please, God,* I kept praying. *Please let him walk through that door.* I thought if he came, it would mean he wasn't 100 percent done with our marriage. That a piece of him still cared.

Larry and I sat off in a corner of the room and talked. He tried to console me, but all I could think of was what I had thrown away, all that I had lost. I wasn't sure there was any hope left in me.

And then I saw him. I gasped and stood up, even though Larry was in the middle of a sentence. He turned and saw Matt. He gave me a quick hug and said his good-byes. He knew who I really wanted to talk to.

Before I knew it, Matt had engulfed me in a bear hug. We both shook with sobs. Disbelief, sadness, despair coursed through our bodies. So much had happened since I'd seen him, since I'd touched him. The accident, Madison, my realizations at rehab. I knew he was carrying a lot holding down the fort at home for Gavin, working, and visiting Madison in the ICU. I wanted to ask how she was, how Gavin was, how he was. There was so much and yet I didn't know how to start.

When we pulled back, both drying our eyes, I saw Matt still wasn't wearing his ring. Before I knew what I was doing, I grabbed his hand and kissed it. "Put it back on," I pleaded, desperately. I held his palm to my face, letting my tears wash it in my love. He pulled his hand away. "I have to go," he said.

Why? He just got here. There was so much I wanted to say, to ask. But I didn't feel like I could push. I was grateful for just his presence. It meant more than I could say.

"Will you be back?" I asked quietly, staring at his hand that I still held in both of my own. He looked at me, tears filling his eyes.

"I don't know," he whispered.

He pulled his hands from mine and began to walk away.

God, if you could take me from this, if you could wake me up from this nightmare, anything, tell me this isn't happening. But I knew that I deserved this torture.

I ran back to my room, hoping that my roommates wouldn't be there, for a moment of quiet. As I entered the empty room, all the emotion of the past two weeks spilled out of me. I threw myself on the bed, tears streaming down my face, my body trembling from the despair that spilled from the deepest part of my soul. Matt was my heart, my love, my best friend. How had I let things get to this point? How had I let him down? I clutched the standard-issue, thinly woven blanket in my hands for support, wishing that the blanket could somehow console me, could somehow ease my ache.

I dropped to my knees in desperation. Without my family, I had nothing. Nothing. I hated who I was, who I had become, how I had allowed myself to become like my own father. But even worse. While he was never around, he'd never almost killed me. Killed my spirit maybe, but he never put me in harm's way.

Why, God, why? Why did I live? I can't face the shame. I can't face this pain. Please, God. Please. I didn't know what I was praying for. But I knew that I was at the end of my rope.

I was spent, had no more tears left inside. As my shoulders stopped shaking and my tears quieted, I felt an overwhelming sense of calmness and warmth. Almost like an embrace you get from a loved one or a friend you haven't seen for a long time, the weight of their arms wrapped around you and the tender squeeze to let you know you've been missed.

Then I heard a voice, like someone talking, though it seemed to be coming from inside. *Get up. It's going to be okay. If you get up and if you trust me, then I will help you through this. But you can't lie on the floor, throwing yourself a pity party. You have to get up.*

Before I knew what was happening, I was lifted off my knees and was sitting on the bed. I was taking deep breaths, feeling the cleansing air coursing through my lungs. And I began to see myself through others' eyes. But not with the disgust and shame I had expected. I was looking through the eyes of my children and I felt their desperation and longing for me to get better and come home. I saw myself through the eyes of my husband wondering where his beautiful bride had gone. I saw my mother's love for me, her grief that I had followed in the footsteps of my father, her hopes that I could overcome the past and be her little girl again.

It's going to be okay. But you have to get up. The words echoed in my mind. Yes, I had messed up. Yes, I was a despicable person. But whether it was God or my guardian angel, someone knew where this was going. That I would make it. But I couldn't lie there anymore.

Never one to believe much in spirituality, in that moment, I was transformed. While I was crying, I was as low as I had ever been, wishing I had been killed in the car crash, yet in the next moment, I had faith. Faith to believe I would make it through this horrible tragedy. That there was a reason I was spared.

I looked around the room and thought about my drinking, my marriage, and the accident. Maybe it was necessary. Maybe it was part of a plan. It brought me to this place so I could start again.

CHAPTER 22 *Matt*

I walked into school. My mom and Amy's mom were kind enough to be staying with Madison at the hospital while I returned to work. I hated the fact that everyone knew my dirty business. They knew what I was dealing with, that Amy had driven drunk and injured our kids and that she was now at rehab. I couldn't even look any of my colleagues in the eye. I wondered why I had the only fucked-up life in the world. Everyone around me knew I was some sort of loser.

Some of my fellow teachers had started a group that would cook meals for me to take home at night. I appreciated the food and the fact that I wouldn't have to scrounge something up for Gavin and me after I visited Madison at the hospital after work. But it still reminded me of the fact that everyone thought I was a failure as a husband and a father.

First period started in fifteen minutes, but I hadn't been to my mailbox in days. I rushed down the hallway, planning to pick up my mail and sort it at my desk before the kids started filtering in. A big stack awaited me. I grabbed the envelopes and papers and headed to my classroom.

Slamming my heavy bag down on the floor, I collapsed into my chair and started to sift through the papers. Flyers for fundraisers, notices about new lunch policies. Then a blank envelope. I ran my finger under the flap and peered inside to see a stack of twenty-dollar bills.

I pulled them out, confused, and began to count. $20, $40, $60. It kept going. $800. No note. No nothing.

As the initial shock began to wane, I slumped back in my chair.

Then I put my head in my hands.

My colleagues had pulled together a collection for me.

While I was stunned with their generosity and floored by the effort, deep down all I felt was shame.

Of course everyone knew how difficult this time was. Everyone knew that I had long been a planner, stashing away money since I was in my early twenties, eager to build a strong retirement fund so that I could enjoy my later years with my wife, traveling, maybe buying a beach house, and having the grandkids come visit. Of course my marriage was in shambles, so I couldn't see that ever happening. But even more painful was how much debt we were in.

I'm a teacher, and my salary alone could never cover the mortgage on our house. But one of the reasons I married Amy was her professional drive. She'd even started a master's program years ago, and I knew she always planned to work. None of us planned for her to be unemployed for two years. I just didn't make enough to pay off our credit cards and pay the mortgage. My colleagues didn't know it, but my two credit cards had a combined balance of $80,000.

In many ways, I was as ashamed of this as I was of my wife.

The bell rang and I had to shake myself out of my misery. I quickly stuffed the envelope into my bag, wondering how on earth I would ever thank them, let alone acknowledge what they'd done for me.

CHAPTER 23 *Amy*

I *didn't know exactly what had happened* in my room that afternoon Matt walked away, but I knew I was different. Some people say God enters your heart, some people say you're saved. All I know is I finally felt like I had the faith to try to heal. That I no longer wanted to give up.

I knew the healing process wasn't going to be easy. I was scared to see the truth. Nobody wants to see the bad in themselves. I had spent the better part of two decades pointing my finger in every direction but my own.

Healing meant accepting responsibility. Yes, it was difficult to own up to what I'd done, but it also meant regaining my power. Taking the power away from the drink or my circumstances and saying *Amy, this is your chance. Like the voice said, you have to get up off that floor.*

After twenty-one days, I was nervous to go home. Madison was out of the hospital and resting comfortably at home. I couldn't wait to see her. I couldn't wait to see both of my children. But I couldn't deny that rehab provided me shelter. A respite from the repercussions of my actions. I was afraid to see my kids. Afraid to face Matt's anger and disappointment day in and day out.

Matt came to collect me around 6:00 in the evening. Anxious and unsmiling, he looked like someone who'd been called in the middle of the night to bail their annoying cousin out of jail. Like he wanted to be anywhere but here.

I followed Matt to the car with a few people I had befriended during my stay. We gathered alongside the passenger side of the truck, grabbing hands and praying together. I was praying for strength, they were praying for my survival. I gave hugs good-bye and that was it. I was headed home. But was it my home? Could I still call it home? Matt was still not wearing his wedding ring. Any day the police could arrive on my doorstep and take me away.

As we settled in for the drive home, I asked some questions, hoping to pull Matt out of his stupor. What had they been doing for the last month? How was Madison healing?

Matt focused on the road. "Slow, but she's a fighter," he said. "But of course she's frustrated being stuck at home. No kinder-garten and no play dates."

Matt just had to throw that in there. Like I didn't feel bad enough.

When we pulled into the driveway, I could barely keep myself from opening the door and running up to the house, excitement and nerves churning in my stomach.

Finally, Matt parked and I jumped out of the car. I cracked open the door leading into the mudroom and peaked around the door. No one. I stepped inside and shut the door behind me. Still no one. I slowly walked through the laundry room to the kitchen, butterflies swirling in my stomach to the point of nausea. My thoughts started to race, and I was kicking myself for expecting a grand welcoming. I mean, who was I kidding? Look at what I had just put my family through!

I walked through the kitchen and there they were, sitting on the couch, watching cartoons, my mom on the couch next to them. "Hi guys," I said, quietly.

Their heads spun around and eyes lit up. "Mommy!" they yelled simultaneously, Gavin running to engulf me in a huge hug, my mom having to hold Madison back, reminding her to stay sitting on the couch. I picked up Gavin and walked over to Madison so she could join the reunion.

Matt came in a few seconds behind me, but we didn't notice. The three of us sat on the floor of the living room wrapped in each other. *This is what I expected,* I thought. *This is what I needed.* My kids. Their love. Their forgiveness. Tears trailed down my cheeks, wetting their hair. With every tear spilled regret, sadness, despair, love, and deep down, hope.

● ● ●

While rehab was a beginning, I knew the hard work started now, at home, faced with all the problems that had caused me to drink in the first place. I wanted Matt to know that I was frustrated with myself for letting my addiction get so out of control. I wanted him to know how envious I was of his being able to enjoy alcohol and not have it consume his life. And that I had committed to not making booze the only answer for me anymore.

I knew I had to change, but how? How was I going to stop "it"? There were so many mornings I had promised myself I wasn't going to drink that day then found a beer in my hand before noon. So how was this time going to be different from all of the other times? *Me, sober, yeah right.* This is where the hard work would begin. This is where I needed to believe that it was possible.

But Matt and I had hardly said two words to each other since I'd gotten home. I understood his anger and his silence. But I knew I was going to need a partner to stay strong. That if I was going to get better, we were going to have to address the issues in our marriage.

But how could I push it? I was the one who'd gotten us into this mess. I was lucky he was even letting me stay in the house, let alone in his bed. So I tiptoed around him. Head down, eyes averted. Trying to show him that I realized how wrong I had been.

About a week after I got out of rehab, Matt was late coming home from work. He said that he had "something" to do. He always had something to do since I'd been home. He was avoiding me.

Finally, around 6:30 he came in the door and plopped down on the couch beside me. I was surprised. Usually he kept his distance, both physically and emotionally.

He looked tired and glanced nervously over his shoulder into the kitchen. My mom was there with the kids, finishing up dinner.

"I went to a lawyer," he blurted out. His eyes were sad and his voice shaky. I didn't respond. I knew I had a slew of legal battles ahead of me but I thought Matt knew about the lawyer my father had hired.

"A divorce lawyer," he said softly, when he could tell I didn't understand. Before I knew what was happening or that my mom could overhear the conversation, she was there at my side. I said nothing. While I knew he wasn't wearing his wedding ring, that I had betrayed him more times than I could count, in the back of my mind I never truly believed that he would divorce me. I wanted to think we were indestructible. I knew now we weren't.

I could tell this was hard for Matt, but he was trying to keep his cool, to be all business. "Here's how this is going to work," he said. "You are going to move out, leave the kids with me, sign your rights over, and just walk away," he said, matter of fact. Before the words could sink in, my mother stepped in front of him.

"Over my dead body," she shouted, her petite frame tensed with anger, trying to block me from his words. "She is not leaving her children."

Matt looked up at my mom, his eyes cold. "No, she just almost kills them."

I squeezed my eyes shut, wishing it were a dream. *Wake up, wake up, wake up,* I screamed silently in my mind. But when I opened my eyes, there I was, facing the repercussions I'd wanted to avoid.

I didn't argue with him. I didn't ask any questions. I just sat there, letting the reality of what I'd done wash over me again.

• • •

I still can't believe I didn't drink the night Matt told me he wanted a divorce. But I think the shock had numbed me enough that I didn't need the drink. But the next day, when Matt still wasn't home, the kids were at my mom's and I was home alone? I couldn't avoid the feelings. And I went right back to the solution that had been so trustworthy all along.

There was still alcohol in the house. I don't know why we hadn't gotten rid of it. I felt like Matt left it there to test me. He knew I was going to relapse. He didn't believe in my sobriety. So why not dangle it there, waiting for me to screw up?

The cold bottle felt so good in my hands, the quiet swish of the liquor like a promise. Should I do it? Did it even matter anymore, if Matt was going to divorce me? How would I live without him, without the daily smiles of my children?

I placed the bottle to my lips and without so much of a pause started swigging. It didn't take long to finish what was left in the bottle and for the reality of what I had just done to set in. I sat there in disbelief of how quick it all went down. Staring at the empty bottle of Captain, taunting me, my disease laughing at how weak I was, I sat and cried.

• • •

Two hours later I was drunk and calling my sister-in-law, telling her I was coming over. Though she was no longer married to my brother, Joe, she never turned me away. She was the closest thing I had to a sister, and I felt like I needed someone. Someone I could rely on.

But as soon as I arrived, she could tell I was drunk and confronted me with her suspicions. "Who do you think you are?" I yelled. "How dare you suggest that I've been drinking," I shouted, indignant even as I slurred the words.

She went to get her phone and I knew she was going to call Matt. I ran upstairs into the bathroom, slamming the door behind me. I don't know what I thought I could escape by locking myself in there. And in there, I was trapped with the one person I wanted to escape. Me.

I stood there looking at my reflection in the mirror.

How could you be so stupid as to drink again? I scolded the woman who stared back at me. *What is wrong with you?!* I wanted to scream. The longer I stood in front of the mirror, the less I saw of the confident, charismatic woman I had once been and more and more of the reckless drunk I had become. Who was this person? What happened to Amy? Where did she go?

Then I heard Matt, knocking on the door of the bathroom.

I didn't even try to hide the slur of my words. Let him know he caused this. He did this to me. His wife is a fuck-up because he withholds his love.

Shut up, I wanted to scream at him as he berated me for my actions, for my weakness. *Shut up shut up shut up!* I knew everything he was saying. I said it to myself every day. Why did he feel the need to punish me further? Didn't he know the hell that I lived in every day in my head?

But he didn't. Or he didn't care. No one did. Life would be better if I just weren't here anymore. For me. For Matt. For my kids.

I pulled open the medicine cabinet and began grabbing every pill I could find. Over the counter drugs, prescription drugs, cough syrup, it didn't matter. I cupped them in my hands and poured them in my mouth, washing them down with my beer. Again, another handful, another drink.

I hated myself. I hated feeling like a failure. I was frantic. I reached into my bag and pulled out the Klonopin I was prescribed and finished what was left in the bottle. If I could just go to sleep. If I could just sleep. I wept as I pulled my knees to my chest and waited for my shaking body to stop. Despondent and cursed by an addiction, I lay on the floor, in agony of who I was. I wanted it all to go away. I just wanted to sleep.

CHAPTER 24 *Matt*

I *knocked on the door with no response.*

"Amy!" I shouted. "Come on!"

Though deep down I wished she'd lock herself in there and never come out.

I leaned my head against the cold wood of the door and thought of Gavin and Madison waiting at home, hoping to have dinner with their parents, for some semblance of normal in the chaos of what their life had become. Though there was no way Amy was coming home like this. I'd make Christine keep her or call Amy's mom to pick up her mess of a daughter. *Here we go again,* I thought.

I heard the click of the lock and Amy pushed past me. I turned to look in the bathroom and saw the pill bottles littering the sink and floor.

She did it. She really did it this time.

Another mess to clean up. But not this time. I was numb to what she had done. I didn't want her to affect me anymore.

I turned on my heel, bolted down the stairs, and grabbed my keys on the counter, ignoring Christine trying to comfort Amy in the kitchen.

"Whatever, I don't care if you die, I'm leaving!" I yelled over my shoulder as I slammed the front door shut. The cold air did nothing to shock me out of my rage. I jumped into my car and pulled away.

As I sped toward home, toward my two kids who needed both their mom and dad, my head was spinning. I couldn't stop playing out what would happen if Amy died. This nightmare would be over. I wouldn't have to keep worrying about my kids being safe. I wouldn't have to return each night in fear of what I would find. I wouldn't have to face a very messy, public divorce, an embarrassing public trial. Everything would be . . . easier.

PART FIVE

Recovery

*The past is gone, the future is not here, and
right now we are free of both.*

—Deepak Chopra

CHAPTER 25 *Amy*

"*Dear Lord, please, heal her.* Bring her back to us, and take away this demon that still has a hold on her. . . ."

"Lord, please guide us. . . ."

"Please, God, please . . ."

The prayers floated over me as I tried to open my heavy eyelids. *Where was I?* I recognized the sound of my mom's voice. Then I heard Matt's mom. That made a bit more sense. Maybe she'd convinced my mom to pray because . . . *Wait, who was that? Why are my eyelids as heavy as boulders?* I was straining to look around, to see where I was. I couldn't focus. Every time I attempted to open my eyes, I was met with this forcing bright light that would drive my eyes back shut.

The third voice, light, soft, kind. Mary. My friend. While we'd only gotten together a couple of times since I'd left rehab, I recognized her voice.

But never would I have expected these three women to be in the same room.

I felt myself drifting off again but I pulled myself back. I wracked my brain, trying to remember where I was, what I'd done today. I felt the familiar pangs of a hangover in my limbs, but this was different. I didn't feel drunk, I felt exhausted, like my body had tried to run a marathon.

I saw Christine's face and remembered going to her house. The bottle of Captain at home. Matt and his angry words flashed before me. He was disappointed in me yet again.

And then it came back to me. The pills. The cold bathroom floor. My last cry for help. But what had I done? I didn't really want to die. My kids. Even though I was a sorry excuse for a mother, they needed a mom. Why couldn't I get my act together, be the mother they both deserved?

The first time I ever thought of killing myself was in high school. I was a senior. To everyone else, I had it all together, and on the outside, I did. But on the inside I was hurting, bad. I thought about it: how I would do it, who would miss me, and would anyone even notice? I scared myself into thinking that there was something wrong with me for having these thoughts, so I would push them away. I buried them deep down where no one could see. The truth was that I didn't want to die; I just didn't want to feel like shit anymore. I was tired of feeling rejected, confused, and unloved. I was tired of hurting and being depressed. The damage to my psyche was done long before I ever picked up a drink. Drinking was just how I managed my thoughts and emotions every day after.

As self-pity and my poor-me refrain began to wash over me, I heard someone else.

Wake up.

I tried to pull my eyes open again, but nothing.

Wake up.

Still nothing. Who was this? It felt like a dream. It was different from the voices of my family. It wasn't male or female. It seemed to be coming from inside my head. But instead of the words I was used to hearing, the berating, mean, self-deprecating comments, this voice was soothing, calm. It captivated me.

And then it spoke again:

Get up, Amy. I'm still here and I will help you through this.

I strained to listen, to remember this voice and discover where it was coming from. I knew this voice. I had heard it before. But where? Then it came to me. This was the voice I'd heard in rehab. Was it God? My angel? I still didn't know. But slowly, I opened my eyes and began to pray with Mary, Loretta, and my mother.

Those three women grabbed onto me and prayed over my tired and terrified body. I clutched their hands begging for a miracle. Mouthing the Our Father and Hail Mary along with them and eventually out loud, we prayed in the ER, unwavering in our faith and absolute in our convictions that we needed a miracle. Nothing else would do.

As my body began to shake, from the emotions pouring out of me, from feeling the depth of their love, and the depth of my need, I had one thought: *This disease is powerful.* I wasn't sure how I would survive another one of its attacks. I was convinced that I wouldn't. I needed to surrender.

• • •

I was released from the hospital later that evening, shocked that the doctor hadn't pushed when he asked whether I meant to take all those pills and I said no, an obvious lie. I don't know why he believed me—I had obviously attempted suicide. But he didn't push the matter. If he had, I knew that the Department of Family Services would have been called and I would have been sent back to rehab or worse, lost my children, for sure.

Instead, Matt brought me home to my father-in-law sitting on the living room floor with the kids playing Candyland. Everyone just looked at me. Denny, the kids, Matt; no one knew what to say. I felt like a stranger. I felt like a traitor. I had to get out of there.

I went upstairs and called Mary. "I need a meeting," I said, trying to keep the desperation out of my voice.

"I'll be right there," she replied, her tone warm and soothing.

I knew having a friend in the program was a key part of success. You were supposed to have someone to call on whenever you were feeling tempted or weak. But I was never good at asking for help. That's what had gotten me into this mess in the first place. The fact that she had been in the hospital and seen me at my weakest? It made me realize that maybe she really did want to be there for me.

As I saw her car pull into the driveway, snow began to fall.

"Come on, let's go find someplace warm to talk," she said as I got into her passenger seat.

I didn't know what to say. But I knew she must have something to share. Something to help.

She kept her eyes on the road.

"The first thing you need to know is I'm going to love you until you can love yourself again."

I don't know why, but those words melted something hard and cold in my heart. I hadn't even realized how much of a wall I had erected over the years. How hardened I had become. It had been a long time since anyone had said anything remotely kind to me. Who could blame them? I was a horrible person. But to hear that she was going to not only help me but love me? She didn't even know me.

If it were anyone else, I would've brushed them off, thought they were full of shit and clichés. But not Mary. There was just something about her that I trusted. She was for real and she was going to help me.

She talked fast but I listened to her share her own struggles with alcohol and I paid attention to the parts I could relate to the most: the husband, the children, the job. I listened to her pour her heart out to me with encouragement and honesty. I listened as she told me the secrets and shame of her path, the hurt and the pain we cause during our drinking and the remorse and embarrassment we feel afterward.

Then she paused, letting the words of her story sit in the air.

"There is a softer, easier way," she said, her voice barely above a whisper.

I turned to her, tears welling in my eyes. She grabbed my hand and smiled, the warmth of both immediately soothing my frozen hands and spirit. "You don't have to feel like this anymore."

I turned and looked out the window. I had barely noticed how hard it had started to snow. The scene reminded me of a galactic voyage in a *Star Wars* movie. Our ship was approaching warp speed with all the dots of snow coming straight at us like spears. We became fixated on the white snowflakes zooming toward us. We looked at each other and laughed at how crazy we were to be out on the road in this kind of weather. We laughed at the irony of the situation. Would we go to any lengths to get sober? *Um, . . . I think so.* We were willing to drive in a blizzard just because we needed the comfort of another booze aficionado to warm our souls and savor the beauty of friendship. I hadn't laughed like that in a long time and it felt good.

CHAPTER 26 *Matt*

I *turned the handle of the garage door,* already hearing a ruckus inside. But it wasn't the typical ruckus of Amy yelling or something being smashed to the floor. This was . . . laughter. I plopped my keys on the kitchen counter to discover an intense tickle war happening on the floor between Amy and Gavin. Madison was propped up on the couch, watching with glee, clearly wishing she could be a part of the action.

I couldn't help it. I smiled.

Amy looked up and met my eye. I tried to shake the smile away, but she had already seen it.

Ever since her trip to the ER, since that moment when she wanted to die, and I wanted her dead, something had shifted. She was meeting with Mary regularly, going to meetings, starting to work out again. When I got home from work, I was no longer met with the kids parked in front of the TV. Instead, I saw Amy helping with homework and dinner on the stove. It was starting to feel like . . . normal. Well, a normal that I could hardly even remember. But it was . . . nice.

But I still didn't trust Amy. I was almost infuriated by these good days because I knew a bad day was around the corner, and it would hurt that much more if I allowed myself to get my hopes up.

We were living in the same house but as complete strangers. Two ghosts who couldn't see the other. I didn't allow her to go anywhere with the kids. She could only see them if she stayed in the house. I was just waiting for the phone call. The call when the police would ask Amy to come in for booking, for the official charges. Driving under the influence. Child endangerment. Amy had hired a lawyer to fight the charges, but, no matter how good he was, she would serve time. I remembered the state trooper's eyes when he talked about his own brush with a drunk driver. "She will not go unpunished." So I knew it was just a matter of time. And I couldn't wait. I just wanted her out of our house and out of our lives.

Deep down I also knew that I was waiting to file for divorce until the charges were official. I still harbored some hesitation about divorce because it was such a foreign thing for my family. But no one could blame me for divorcing someone who was headed to jail, right?

• • •

One Saturday morning while the kids were wrapped up in morning cartoons, still in their pajamas, enjoying a lazy family weekend, Amy knocked on my office door.

I waved her in, not saying anything.

"What's up?" I said, my voice clipped.

She was holding something in her hand and she looked on the verge of tears.

"I think I'm pregnant," she said.

Oh come on, now this? What, did she think I was stupid? There's no way she was pregnant. Another lie, I thought. *Another ploy to get sympathy.*

But I wasn't falling for it this time.

Amy had always wanted another child. But I didn't. We weren't using protection and hadn't been since Madison's birth, but I knew the chances were slim. Amy had had a colonoscopy earlier that year, and they'd discovered in the process that her left fallopian tube had fused shut and her uterus was displaced. It was highly unlikely that we'd be able to have another child. I remember how devastated Amy was by the news, but I had felt validated that two children was the right number for us. Case closed.

But I knew why she was bringing this up. If we had another child, she thought I wouldn't divorce her. She wanted to rein me back in.

"Whatever, I don't believe you," I finally said in response.

"Well, I'm late and I took two tests. The first one had two faint lines, see? The second one didn't, but I still think I'm pregnant."

I grabbed the test from her hand and threw it in the trash.

"Well, I'm sure it isn't mine," I said as I walked out the door.

Boom! Another grenade thrown in her face. In the few conversations we'd had about rehab, she'd talked about how some people snuck in drugs and had sex, even though it was against the rules. I didn't really think Amy had done that, but I knew saying that would hurt her. And I still wanted to hurt her as much as possible. I still wanted her to pay for all we were going through, all we had gone through for the past two years, and for what it had been like to fear that my child might be taken from me because of her stupidity and selfishness.

I walked up the stairs to our bedroom, thinking I'd escape into the shower and not have to deal with her.

But as the hot water coursed over my body, reality set in. I had to admit there was a chance she was telling the truth. There was one stupid night after she got back from rehab that I allowed myself to give in to my needs. She'd been gone a month, I'm a guy, and she was a warm body in my bed at night.

I shook my head. *What if it was true? Why now? Right when I was about to be free from her?*

I felt sick. How would my parents react? They were so committed to getting Amy out of my life and especially the kids' lives. Despite their Catholic values, they had even offered to pay for the divorce lawyer. That's how much freedom from Amy meant to them. And now this? They would know how weak I was, that I'd allowed her to touch me in that way, to create this life.

Shame washed over me. My one-time need for physical satisfaction might have bound me to Amy yet again.

CHAPTER 27 *Amy*

When Matt *brushed me off* about the pregnancy, I didn't blame him. I could see how it looked, and he still didn't trust me. I had had pregnancy scares before and they never panned out. But when I still hadn't gotten my period two weeks later, I decided to call my doctor. Maybe it was stress, maybe it was all the things going through my body since my OD. But deep down, I was holding out hope that this was a miracle.

Matt and I were always on the fence about a third child . . . meaning I wanted one and he didn't. When we found out that conceiving again was highly unlikely, it broke my heart. I don't know why, but I just felt like I wasn't complete. It felt like something was missing from our family.

My doctor wanted me to come in immediately. I was on Cymbalta for my depression and, if I was pregnant, he wanted me to stop taking it immediately.

As I sat in the lab, waiting for the test results, my palms were sweating. But I knew what the results would be. I just knew I was pregnant.

The phlebotomist came out smiling and handed me the printout of my results. "Congratulations," he said. The sheet of paper indicated my HCG levels were high, meaning . . . I was definitely pregnant.

"Thank you," I managed to get out before I ran out to the car to call Matt. I tried to calm myself before dialing his number. Containing my own excitement out of fear of his response, when he answered the phone I simply said, "Positive."

Dead silence. "Well, there it is," he finally said. And promptly hung up. I sat in the driver's seat of my car and burst into tears. I didn't even know what I was feeling. Shock and excitement about the baby. Sadness and despair at how things were with Matt. Then it hit me: how was I going to have a baby, when I could be going to jail? And for who knows how long? I knew child endangerment, driving under the influence, and reckless driving held stiff consequences.

I kept thinking about all of those drunken nights when we didn't use protection and were careless, all of those nights we were too caught up in the moment to care about the outcome, any one of those tender nights we playfully considered another child, but nothing. Nothing ever came of those nights. The nights our relationship was good and loving and strong. When Matt had looked at me with love in his heart and lust in his eyes, the nights we were passionate about "us."

I remembered all those years I spent secretly wanting another baby but was met with disappointment each month. *Why now?* I thought, *why now after all that has happened? Why after six years of nothing? Why would I get this amazing gift? And now, in the midst of my despair? How could I receive this wonderful present that I did not deserve?*

• • •

A few weeks later, we still hadn't spoken about the news. I knew I shouldn't have been surprised. We'd hardly been speaking at all. But I still felt like the news that we were having another baby warranted . . . something.

Then Matt came in one weekend from mowing the lawn, sweaty and red in the face. He was opening the mail and I could see that he was frustrated. The mail was always a low point. We weren't making enough to cover our expenses and with each passing month our debt grew. I couldn't help but feel responsible and he didn't hesitate to remind me of that fact.

As he opened one envelope after another, his anger mounted. Before I knew it, his fury flew like daggers. "Where are we supposed to come up with money to pay this bill?" he ranted, "or this one, or this one?" he listed as he threw each envelope on the counter in front of me.

I was taken aback. I'd been so used to radio silence from him I hardly knew how to respond. But what did he want me to say? I knew we were in trouble.

I resorted back to my typical coping mechanism. Turn it back on him. "Well, get a part-time job!" I said, throwing up my hands. Who did he think he was? I had gotten a job as soon as I could. There weren't many places that would hire me, but I found a job providing respite care for adults with children with special needs. It was an exhausting job, one no one else wanted to do, but it kept me busy and it helped contribute something to the bills.

"Oh, come on, Amy. We wouldn't be in this position if it weren't for *you*! You ruined *my life*!" Matt cried out.

I just stood there. The look on his face said it all. This wasn't just a comment made in anger. No, in a split second it had turned into something more than that. I could see it on his face and I could hear it in his voice. He was beaten. His ego whitewashed for everyone to see. This was too much for him, and he'd reached his breaking point. His eyes filled with tears and he said it again only this time softer and sad. "You ruined my life."

I knew he was telling the truth. I did ruin his life, or at least a portion of it. All the planning and savings he was so proud of were gone. Everywhere he went, people talked. Just as I tried to lock myself in the house to avoid the derision of the community,

Matt still had to face it every day as he went to work or went to the gym. He tried to hang out with friends, at least those who would still have him. Most of Matt's friends stayed away, out of his drama. They didn't want to be associated with a drunk.

I couldn't argue with him. I stood there letting his words penetrate. I had no defense against them. I knew he was right. I followed him out to the garage where I found him sitting on our old couch crying. I didn't know whether to go to him or stay where I was and give him space.

"What do you want?" he said to me with his head still in his hands. He couldn't even look at me.

"I'm sorry," I said. I knew it wasn't much. But it was all that I had.

I stood there watching my big strong husband cry and whimper like a broken little child. *This is what I have reduced him to*, I thought.

But he didn't want to hear it. He was hurt and angry at what our life had become; he was grieving the loss of the old Matt and Amy and didn't know how either of us fit in our new roles: me an alcoholic and him the spouse to one.

Matt told me to go inside, but I just stood there. I didn't want to walk away and lose my chance to get close to him. Maybe this was finally the moment where we could talk. Where I could get my husband back.

"Tell me what I can do to fix this," I said softly. "Tell me what I can do to show you I'm sorry," I pleaded.

Matt looked up at me and the child growing inside me and let out a small chuckle of disbelief. He pointed at my stomach. "You've done enough."

I looked at him in shock. "You're not suggesting I got pregnant on purpose, are you?"

"It wouldn't surprise me," he said in a matter-of-fact tone, like he was telling me the score of the softball game, not insinuating that I was a manipulative, conniving slut.

But he wasn't done. "How am I going to explain that," he said, pointing at my stomach, "to my parents, my friends, everyone that told me to get the hell away from you?" He paused. "You almost kill our first two, now you're having another one," he blurted out. "What are people going to think?" He shook his head. The anger was gone. In its place was defeat.

I still stood in the doorway of the garage, fighting back tears with everything I had in me. He was not going to see me cry.

"I guess you'll tell them the truth," I said. I didn't know what he wanted me to say or do, so I just kept standing there. We stayed silent for a while, staring into nothing and waiting for the other one to speak. Finally, I asked him what had been burning inside my heart since the day I had ruined everything, the words I didn't think I deserved to hear the answer to but I was desperate for, like water to my dehydrated soul.

"What will it take to get things back on track?" I whispered. "How can I get you to love me again?"

Deep down I still hoped that Matt might give us another chance. Move forward with our lives together, with the new baby, with a new "us." But Matt wasn't attracted to this Amy. He wanted the old Amy. The one who worked out, knew how to have fun, and walked confidently into any room.

"I just want my old Amy, my bride back," he said, resigned, but honest.

I took a few steps toward him. "Give me time, please. You'll see her again, I promise."

But Matt shook off my answer, getting up off the coach. "I can't make any promises," he said. His voice had changed. No longer defeated, I felt like he was gearing up for another fight.

"I don't know if I still love you." He paused, seeming to be finished, and then added, "Get a hobby, find something that makes you happy." He paused again, really thinking about his answer. "Go back to school and finish your degree. Do something with your life," he pleaded. And then finally, "Lose some weight. The girl I knew would never have let herself look like this."

I clenched my jaw. Nodded. Then turned and walked back inside. As I walked through the door to the mudroom, I started to cry. I just couldn't hold it in anymore.

Maybe Matt felt that he was a little too harsh with his words because he followed me in. I felt Matt grab the back of my arm and he turned me around. He pulled me in close to him and hugged me.

I clung to him like a lifeline. Desperate for his touch, this hug that had been my home for the past ten years. We held each other tight and cried. There was nothing left, we were both emotionally bankrupt and literally had nothing left to do but cry. Neither of us was sure how we were going to get through this.

I knew in my heart that he needed to say those things to me, whether he truly believed them or not. I could have allowed myself to get hung up on the words that he used. But I knew. Matt wasn't calling me fat, lazy, or boring. He was crying out. In his own way, he was grieving and trying to hold on to the only thing he knew. He didn't know sober Amy or sober "Matt and Amy." His words may have been get a hobby, go to school, and lose some weight, but his heart was asking, *Who is this new person, what is life going to be like with you, and will I ever see my bride again?*

He pulled out of the embrace and walked out to his car. I heard the engine start and his truck pull out of the garage. Though my heart still hurt from his words, the memory of his touch still lingered on my limbs. I closed my eyes, holding on to his embrace in my mind. I didn't know if it might be the last time he ever hugged me.

CHAPTER 28 *Matt*

"*You ruined my life!*"

The words echoed in my head as I sped down the highway, trying to race from my life and my problems. But I knew they were on my tail. That I'd never shake them.

How did this happen?

I mean, I knew how it happened, but I just couldn't figure out why on earth God would allow all of this. The accident. The debt. The baby. I knew Amy saw this baby as a godsend. I saw it as a ball and chain.

I felt like everything in my life was ruined. I'd been hiding out, avoiding friends ever since the accident, not wanting to see the pity on their faces as they knew what a wreck my life had become. I didn't want to answer questions about whether we were getting a divorce. And Lord, how would I ever tell people that Amy was pregnant? I knew she would begin to show in a few months' time, but I couldn't even think about that. I was disgusted with myself. How could I have allowed this to happen?

I had had an out. Amy was going to be charged. Gavin and Madison were five and seven, old enough to understand that sometimes parents split up and that it was best for everyone.

But as I pictured the tiny embryo growing inside Amy, I couldn't fathom leaving that little being behind. Trying to share visitations with a newborn. Obviously I was confident I would get sole custody, but was I ready to tackle not only single fatherhood but also raising an infant on my own? While its mother was in jail?

I just couldn't see how any of this would work out.

• • •

As the weeks went by, I continued to distance myself from Amy. I'd go out on the weekends, every weekend night. Amy wasn't going anywhere. She was always home with the kids. So I took the chance to enjoy some freedom. I even left for the whole weekend a couple of times, heading out of town with guy friends.

While in the past Amy would be on my ass about where I was, who I was with, to the point of paranoia, these days she just let me go. She let me have my space. She didn't question me when I got back.

I relished the freedom Amy was giving me. I was still trying to see myself as an almost divorced man. I allowed myself to look at other women. To imagine what it might be like to ask them out, take them on dates. But my imagination never took it much further than that. I just couldn't picture another woman being my wife. Being a stepmom to my kids.

Plus every day, I'd see more and more glimmers of the old Amy. Of the girl I married. I saw it in the effort she was putting into her appearance. I saw it in her interactions with our kids. I saw it as she prepared for the new life growing inside her.

She took care of the kids, was staying home. Some of it was to be with them but I knew that some of it was to escape the glances and whispers in our town. Everyone knew what she had done. Everyone knew what we were waiting for: the charges, a cop car, jail.

Who knew how much time she had left? She wanted to spend that time with her kids. And I appreciated that she was finally thinking of them for once.

But there were times I saw complete despair as well. She looked like a woman who had given up. She knew it was only a matter of time before the authorities came knocking. She had no idea how long she would be separated from her children. She worried about what they would think of their mother being in prison. She never knew if this day would be her last.

These thoughts seemed to focus her. I could hardly believe how loving and nurturing she was being. I had wanted this for my kids for so long. I wanted them to have a mom like the one I saw in front of me.

Before I even realized what was happening, I started coming home earlier and earlier, stopped avoiding her, stopped taking weekend trips with the guys to get out of the house. I felt the anger and bitterness begin to slowly seep out of me as well.

I tried to push the feelings away, but, as I watched her transform before my eyes, I saw glimpses of my bride coming back to me and I began to love her for the mother she was being, the woman she was being. One day after another, the phone call didn't come, and that allowed me to drift further from the idea of divorce and to drift closer toward the possibility of us being the family that I had always wanted. Little by little, I began to worry about her getting that phone call. Little by little, I hoped that call wouldn't come. Slowly I was remembering all of the reasons I had fallen in love with and married Amy.

And as Amy continued to give me space, to let me be, to let me go . . . I think I realized that I didn't want to be let go.

PART SIX
Reconciliation

*Let all bitterness and wrath and anger
and clamor and slander be put away from you,
along with all malice. Be kind to one another,
tenderhearted, forgiving one another,
as God in Christ forgave you.*

—Ephesians 4:31–32, ESV

CHAPTER 29 *Amy*

When I saw how Matt reacted to the news of the baby, I could tell that he might still divorce me. But despite the crushing blow of his reaction, I knew this was my second chance. This baby would never know me as a drunk. This baby would keep me from drinking. This baby was a godsend.

I couldn't believe how much hope I felt despite the fact that my marriage was in shambles, that I was still awaiting sentencing for drunk driving and could possibly go to jail. I could build a life with this baby. Yes, maybe I'd be in jail for the early years of its life. That would be tough. But I just had faith that somehow, this was part of the plan. Somehow, God was in all that was happening.

I shook my head in disbelief. The old Amy would have reacted to Matt's anger with her "poor me" refrain. She would have turned to alcohol or a pill to numb her to the pain. Or she would have tried to fight back, make him feel as bad as she did. But today, I was sitting with the pain and I was okay. I wasn't looking away. I wasn't running from it. I was feeling it but still felt hope.

I realized that my future was likely going to be alone. I had to let go. To be honest, it had been years since I had felt like part of a team. Yes, I still wanted to be married to him. I wanted him to forgive me. But I knew deep down, that, in order for him to forgive me, I needed to forgive myself. And I had a long way to go.

• • •

T. D. Jakes said something very profound about relationships: "If you want to have a loving relationship, be a loving partner." In other words, be the relationship you want. Somewhere after that fight with Matt, when he said I ruined his life, it hit me. You get what you put out. I had always harped on Matt to be more loving or affectionate or to give me the kinds of compliments and attention I was craving. But did I do those things for him? I started thinking about the kind of person I was in a relationship and the kind of person I wanted in a relationship. Am I the kind of person who is caring, honest, respectful, and kind? Those traits are certainly what I expect, but do I contribute these characteristics to my marriage? Was I being what I wanted? The answer was no.

Obviously, being in recovery, I had begun to look at myself, to stop turning away from the pain and masking it and start looking to see what was really going on. But where would I begin? Soul searching doesn't come with a manual.

I began to pray—and not the "please God get me out of this mess" kind of praying. I began a dialogue with God and I would use it daily. On a run, driving to work, before bed, whenever. I didn't start by saying an Our Father or Hail Mary. I simply started talking, to myself, about what I was feeling and I asked for His help. I was uncomfortable at first because I was never the "God" type. I've always believed in God and the church, but I was the kind of person who only went to church on holidays and for weddings. I guess I could say I never thought I needed Him . . . until now. I had to stay sober. For this baby. For any hope for a future.

Staying out of bars and away from alcohol-driven events was easy. Keeping away from booze was not. If you think about how many places you go where alcohol is present, the list is endless. Just because I stopped drinking didn't mean the world stopped turning. Alcohol was everywhere—sporting events, billboards, commercials, magazines. Not to mention birthday parties, christenings, Fourth of July picnics, any picnic, and weddings.

So, I stopped going. I closed myself in and hid from the world. I went nowhere. Weekend after weekend I stayed home reading and spending time with my children. I was rebuilding relationships with them and focusing on the people that mattered. I used their energy for my strength. I did little things at first, like driving a different way to the store so I didn't have to drive by the local bar I went to, unfriending certain people on social networks that I didn't feel were relevant to my life. I stopped going out to Matt's softball games at night so I didn't have to be around alcohol, and, when I felt shaky and unsure, tempted to turn to alcohol, I called Mary. I went to meetings and listened to other women share their stories of struggle. I joined a book club and started exercising regularly.

Then, when ten months had passed and there were still no charges, I started to hope that I might be spared. Could I escape jail time? Could I really have a chance to rebuild my family? I started to feel Matt's attention again. It wasn't huge, but we started looking in each other's eyes. We started talking again. Nothing major. But I relished each morsel of attention he gave me. It felt good, pure, and honest, like building blocks to our family. Finally, the love I was receiving didn't take so much work—it felt natural. We were on our way to being a family again and I was happy at the progress we were all making.

•   •   •

Then one midsummer morning, I woke up to find my children looking out the living room window at our front lawn. I was feeling drowsy from the pregnancy and didn't quite understand what they were discussing. So I went to the window myself and looked out. My heart broke in disbelief. *How can people be so cruel?*

I knew that driving drunk was a horrible decision, and I was prepared for how difficult it would be for me to move forward and forgive myself. But what I wasn't prepared for was looking out my front window at the beer bottles and beer cans my neighbors had thrown on my front lawn sometime during the night. I wasn't prepared for the looks on my children's faces as they looked up at me and wondered, *Were they Mom's?* I wasn't prepared for the sound in my son's voice when he asked me why someone would do this. I wasn't ready for this kind of blatant disrespect in my own home.

I tried to reassure my kids, explain it was just a prank. I gave them a snack and then ran to the bathroom; the door barely shut before tears of shame erupted.

I kept thinking of all the ways I was trying so desperately to prove that I was sorry and that I wanted to make amends. I was crying at all the progress I thought I had made with my sobriety and all the work that I had put into changing people's perception of me. I was weeping for my kids and the reminder it gave them about the accident and what people really thought about their mother.

As I tried to control my sobs, to cry quietly so my children didn't hear, I put my hand on my belly, thinking of the innocent life growing inside. That poor innocent soul whose mother would always be a leper. It truly didn't matter to people what I was doing now, it only mattered what I had done. I would never be anything other than the woman who almost killed her kids.

• • •

On November 12, 2010, eleven months after the devastating accident that should have ruined my life, Hadley Faith was born.

Two weeks early, she was a force to be reckoned with from the start. And with her was born a new chance for our family. I saw it in Matt's face when the doctor allowed him to deliver his baby girl, the shine of joy and delight and awe as the baby girl slipped from my body into his waiting arms.

There is no doubt in my mind. Hadley Faith was our saving grace. She saved our family.

CHAPTER 30 *Matt*

*T*he day *Hadley Faith was born* changed everything. In that moment, as Amy groaned in pain and pushed one final push, as this beautiful, tiny baby girl slipped into my waiting arms, her loud cry firm and determined, my eyes met Amy's. Pure joy at the miracle of life, at the miracle that had happened between us. I don't know when it had happened. But somewhere in the nine months as Hadley was growing in her mama's belly, I had forgiven Amy.

As we hunkered down in those first few weeks with a newborn, exhaustion in our bones with the constant crying and nighttime waking, we were in the new baby bubble. It felt like me and Amy against the world again.

And some of that was because the world was still against us. Everywhere she went, people talked. Our small town was not ready to forgive Amy for what she did, and any time she left the house, which was rarely in that first year, she faced the derision and disgust of people who had once been our friends. I knew that the lawn incident had crushed Amy. I'd come home to see her tearstained face and red eyes. The shame had taken up permanent residence in her heart.

Plus, my family refused to see her. They had been avoiding her in the last year before the accident, not wanting to see what she had become, feeling powerless to help me in my pain. But after Hadley was born, I think we both thought they would come around. That they would see that we were trying to rebuild. But they just couldn't do it. They were too afraid that things would take a turn for the worse again.

I understood their hesitation. We were still waiting to see if charges would be brought against Amy. For all we knew, even with this new life, the authorities could take it all away whenever they wanted.

But they had only a year to bring charges. It was now almost December. That Christmas was especially sweet as we celebrated as a family of five. Amy and I kept looking at each other. I don't know how to describe it except that we knew that this could all be taken away any day. We were not about to take it for granted.

I couldn't believe my change of heart. I had begged that officer to lock her up. Now my prayers had changed. *Please, God, please, let us get this second chance. Spare us the indignity of a legal battle, of jail time.* We both were sorry for what had happened. We both had repented. *Please, God, let us be.*

CHAPTER 31 *Amy*

No phone call. No formal charges. A year had come and gone with nothing.

I didn't know how to explain that, except that it was a miracle.

The miracle of Hadley. The miracle of no charges. I didn't deserve this.

And while Matt and I both rejoiced, deep down, I still felt shame and guilt. I deserved to be in jail. I deserved to be humiliated with a public trial. I had almost killed my kids. Despite my sobriety and recovery, I still, deep down, hated myself.

It didn't help that I was reminded of my mistake everywhere I went. A few weeks after the one-year anniversary of the accident, I was standing on the sidelines during Gavin's football practice when a woman whose son played on the same team approached me. We made small talk about the weather while we waited on the sidelines for our sons to finish up. We had never met so I extended my hand to introduce myself.

"I know who you are," she said.

"Oh, I'm sorry." Assuming we had met at one of Gavin's games, I laughed and tried to explain how "forgetful" I can be during the hectic football season.

"Oh, no," she said with a toss of her hair. "We haven't met before."

I didn't know what to say. Obviously she knew who I was because the entire town was still talking about me, even one year later.

Here it comes, I thought to myself. *What hurtful jab will come my way now?*

I tensed up in expectation. Finally, she turned away from the practice and toward me. My eyes stayed locked on Gavin.

"I heard about the accident when it happened, but I don't judge you."

Was this really happening? Was I really about to have this conversation with a complete stranger in the middle of my son's football practice and with all of the probing ears around me?

She began to tell me about her father and his struggles with alcohol, the verbal abuse, the beating, and the torment that alcoholics bring into a family. I stood there in silence. The woman kept talking until finally a whistle blew, which disrupted her monologue.

Keeping my eyes to the ground, I walked across the field to meet my son, feeling the convicting glances of the other parents every step of the way. My arms folded across my chest, I scurried to collect Gavin and his things. I just wanted to go home.

This was it, now was the time. All that I had learned over the past year had prepared me for this moment. Would I allow that conversation to derail me, to push me back into my pity party, the poor me, everyone hates me and judges me and I should just go crawl into a hole mind-set? "It" wanted me to feel insecure and hopeless. "It" wanted me to think that everyone was against me.

I had a decision to make. I was either going to allow this person, who was probably just being nosy, to affect all of the progress I had made by choosing to think that she was saying, "You, Amy, are just like my father"—or I could consider that she was trying to let me know that she could relate to me on some level because she, too, had been affected by alcoholism. That in her strange way, she was just trying to connect.

Every day was like this for me. Deciding how to perceive people's words and glances. How to interpret the events of my life. Now that I wasn't being charged, I could either continue to punish myself, by believing that the whole world was against me, or I could let go and be free. Where had all this intolerance come from?

It always felt like people were talking about me. No matter where I was or what I was doing, I felt the need to defend myself. The stares, the comments, they were always there confronting me, reminding me, judging me on what I had done. The sad part is, I felt that I deserved them. I knew that I had gotten off easy. And I knew people weren't happy about it. I had accepted that this was how the rest of my life was going to be. A hamster on a wheel that no matter how hard I tried, I was always going to be paying for the choices I had made.

I constantly felt scrutinized by my family, friends, and neighbors. Before long, being sober started to be more about verifying for the cynics around me that I was sorry for my actions and less about me and my well-being. I was so focused on proving to everyone around me how hard I was working on making this better and how committed I was to making amends for my horrible choice, that I started to lose sight of what really mattered: me.

One time I was at a picnic with family and friends, and Hadley had gotten a hold of a Coors Light can and was playing with it. She was just being a toddler, holding it to her mouth, enjoying the coldness of the can against her lips. I don't think anyone else even noticed. But I was mortified. I had to say something. Had to let everyone know that I was uncomfortable, so I made the comment: "Leave it to my kid," then I grabbed the beer can from her grasp and said, "Please, Hadley, don't be like your mother." No one said anything and no one thought it was funny. But this was the only way I knew how to deal with what I thought everyone was thinking. I hated it being the white elephant in the room.

But with every comment I made, every time I reminded people that I hadn't forgotten what happened, I wasn't allowing anyone to move forward, let alone me. We couldn't close the door on the past because I was the one making the comments and retelling the story. Over and over and over again.

In particular, I couldn't let go of how I had failed my children. I'd remember the nights I placed my children into my bed, turned on the television, and walked out of the room. What might they have been thinking those nights I left them alone with only the entertainment of the television and the companionship of each other? What were they thinking of me, their mother, as they watched me leave the room each night to drink with the people I had gathered below them? Madison with her big brown eyes looking up at me and asking softly in her tiny voice, "Can you lay with me for a minute?" But I didn't and I never did.

Did they feel like they were a burden or that they were in the way? Because, looking back, that is how they were treated. How else would they feel? My children knew they were loved because I told them so, but my actions didn't prove that. My actions proved that I said what I needed to say to get what I wanted. When it was time to be left alone so I could drink with my "friends," the words came out that I loved them, but my actions closed them in a room and isolated their lonesome faces for hours.

There were many nights they would sneak down the stairs to watch the excitement and laughter roaring from the rooms below. I can imagine that they were curious and wanted to be a part of what was taking place in their own home and that they wanted to be with their parents. One night, I was in the garage drinking and entertaining a crowd when I saw Gavin peering around the door leading from the laundry room. He wanted to be where the noise was. He wanted his mother. His round soft face so cheerful and pleasant looked hesitant to take another step, yet he was curious enough to enter into the festivities. He saw me sitting in a lawn chair sipping beer from my red plastic cup and ran toward me smiling with his arms extended.

I was annoyed. Annoyed because it had been the second time that evening that Gavin had come down to get me and I responded to him with a cold stern manner as I grabbed his wrist to drag him back inside. Frustrated, I harshly yelled, "Get back in bed!" I never thought to consider his tender feelings or needs. He was confused. What did he do that was so wrong? He turned back to look at me, his face filled with disappointment. I ignored him by pointing up toward the ceiling and firmly disciplined, "Upstairs!" My five-year-old son turned back toward the stairs and walked up alone and put himself back to bed.

Alcoholism strips us of our compassion and empathy and hinders our abilities, not only as spouses but also as parents. We don't choose to be neglectful of our children. The thirst and the need of the insidious disease overpowers us and we no longer are able to function in our roles. But can we ever really exonerate our hearts for the pain we caused our children?

It never occurred to me that I was affecting two innocent lives. Too often Gavin and Madison were trapped in whatever emotional crisis I was going through at the moment, and it was easier for me to tell them to "go play" than try to explain the chaos in our home. If they had witnessed an argument, or a fight, or the police visiting our home, there was never a discussion afterward to explain to them what was happening and why it was happening. I never took the time to sit with my children and help them understand why all this chaos surrounded their family.

The guilt was starting to eat me alive. Every time I had a moment of happiness, I would try to berate myself. *How dare you be happy? Don't you remember what you did?*

· · ·

I sat in bed, reading, flagging pages, underlining sentences. Matt laughed as he lay in bed next to me, as I'd scribble away in the margins. I was reading Deepak Chopra's *The Seven Spiritual Laws of Success* and I couldn't put it down. I'd been reading every kind of spiritual book I could get my hands on these days, desperate to find some wisdom to help me move on. The way I was living was no life at all. I was attending meetings and meeting with Mary, but I knew that wasn't going to be enough to lift the tremendous weight of guilt off my shoulders.

So much had happened, so many miracles, that I felt like my life was starting to shift, that I was merging into this new person. But I was confused about where my guilt, shame, and remorse fit. I didn't know what role they played in my life now that Matt and I were working on our marriage, that Hadley was here. My life was moving in such a positive direction that I wanted to keep that momentum going. So I dove headfirst into my spirituality.

My mom had long been a fan of Oprah and had been telling me to check out her website for months now. I don't know why I'd resisted, but I finally sat down and started to peruse some of the material on her site. It did seem tailor-made for me with content on forgiveness, shame, guilt, recovery. *Click, click, click.* Each page felt even more significant.

Then I discovered a section on her site that read Share Your Story. *Perfect,* I thought, *a chance for me to share my story, unload some of how I am feeling.* I had about a thousand characters to capture the depth of my experience.

It was the first time I had sat down and actually written my entire story. I wrote about the shame of my drinking, the shame of the accident, how I felt shackled to my guilt and unable to see a future of forgiveness or happiness. I wrote that I felt like punishing myself was the only way to show my children that I was sorry for hurting them.

I never thought that anyone would read my ramblings. It was

more of a release to write it all down, post it out there, on the Internet. *Put it out there and then hopefully move on* is what I thought. I assumed my post would be lost out in cyber world and I was just fine with that.

But despite those thoughts, I felt a strange connection while writing the post, a sense of certainty and calmness. It was like a pull or . . . a force was preset, as if I were being led to write it. I felt like something huge was going to come of it. But I had no idea what.

• • •

Just after Hadley's first birthday, a few weeks before Christmas, I was home decorating with my niece and Madison and Hadley when my cell phone rang. I didn't recognize the number. Sigh. These days, it always seemed to be another bill collector reminding us of our debt. I'd gotten into the habit of passing myself off as the sister or babysitter so I didn't have to talk to them.

"Hello?" I said, tentatively.

"May I speak to Amy, please?" said a clear, strong female voice.

"She's not in, may I take a message?" I responded, all business.

"This is Stephanie from Harpo Studios. When do you expect her back?"

Wait . . . HARPO . . . What? As in OPRAH's Harpo?

"Um, she went to the store, she'll be right back," I said. I couldn't just say, *never mind it's me, I just screen my calls in case you're a bill collector.*

"Okay, we'll call back," she said and before I knew it the line was dead.

I stood there, trying to process what had just happened. Hadley was pulling on my leg, trying to get me to pick her up. I swung her into my arms, nose nuzzling into her golden curls as I tried to gather my thoughts. *Were Oprah's people really calling me? For what?*

Then it hit me . . . my post. I remembered the feeling I had when I wrote it. As if it were the beginning of something significant.

Why did I say I was at the store? I was desperate to know what they wanted. I looked at the number on my phone, thinking I'd just call her back. But I couldn't remember her name.

"Harpo Studios, how may I direct your call?"

I paused, trying to wrack my brain yet again for the woman's name. Nothing.

"Hi, yes, I just received a phone call from a woman there. I was hoping to track her down? My name is Amy?" I knew this was a long shot, but I was desperate to get some answers.

"Ma'am, I'm afraid we have over 400 employees working here, so, um, unless you have a name, I don't think I can help you." The man's voice was understanding but firm. When I didn't say anything, he spoke again. "Don't worry, I'm sure they'll call back," he said as he hung up the phone.

Damn it! I could have kicked myself. Why did I do that? I decided to save the number in my phone under "Oprah." If they called back I wouldn't make that mistake again.

But days passed, then weeks. Christmas came and went. Nothing.

Finally, on a cold January afternoon, as I was driving home from work, my phone rang. I looked down to see who it was. The caller ID said OPRAH. I quickly picked up.

It was Stephanie again. And as I'd guessed, she'd read my post and was interested in hearing more about my story.

I couldn't stop myself from shaking in excitement. Someone from Oprah's company had actually read my post, and my words had driven someone to pick up the phone.

"Well, thank you for sharing your story. And I wanted to let you know that we are taping a Lifeclass with Deepak Chopra at the end of the month. We wanted to know if you'd like to attend the session in person."

I couldn't believe my ears. Why was I being rewarded with this opportunity? Although there was no way I would turn it down.

They sent a lengthy questionnaire for me to fill out and return before the session. The questions were partly on Deepak and partly on my story. The last question asked: If you could ask Deepak anything, what would it be? I thought about that one for a long time. Finally, I carefully crafted the essence of what I was still struggling with: How do I begin to move forward, when there is so much guilt holding me back?

When I spoke with Stephanie again to arrange details for the trip to New York City for the live taping, Stephanie had something else to ask.

"Listen, we've been talking a lot about what might make this session really powerful. We'd like you to sit in the front row and ask your question for Deepak personally, during the taping. Is that something you'd feel comfortable doing?"

"Yes!" I could hardly contain my excitement. I knew that this trip, being in the same room with Deepak, having the chance to ask him something so personal, something that could help me move forward in my life in such powerful ways meant that God was truly at work.

Off I went with my mother and my Aunt Bev to New York City. When we arrived at Radio City Music Hall, I was thrilled to discover that I would be seated in the front row, just three seats away from Ms. Gayle King, Oprah's BFF. I couldn't believe this was happening. Here I was, so ashamed of who I was and what I had done, but Oprah's people felt my story of transformation warranted a trip here. To sit on this stage.

As the taping began, the room pulsed with energy. The vibe was unreal, and I knew it was a place of miracles. I felt the energy in the room in my bones, from head to toe. The hour felt like ten minutes and, before I knew it, the taping was over. I hadn't had a chance to ask my question but I knew that I had just had the most amazing afternoon of my life.

I felt that I'd learned the answer to my question. There was a phrase that stuck with me: *The past is gone, the future is not here, and right now we are free of both.*

I knew that meant it was time to let go, it was time to be in the moment of my life again and not look back or worry what tomorrow would bring because right now is all that matters.

The accident happened and that day is gone, I don't know what the future holds, if my marriage is going to survive, if I can stay sober, or what my life might look like two days from now. I can't spend my time worrying about what happened in the past or what will happen tomorrow. I have now, and that should be my focus.

But the conviction began to wane with every day I was at home, and my enthusiasm quickly faded. I couldn't help feeling that I didn't deserve to be happy. Every time I felt an ounce of happiness, I would pause. My mind would scream *Don't you ever forget what you did!* and I was right back to feeling guilty, only this time I was feeling guilty about being happy in the moment. I'd remind myself of what I'd done and I refused to let the past go. I would much rather hold on to my guilt in order to prove that I was sorry, than let it go. For me, merely saying the words "I'm sorry," and truly meaning them just didn't seem enough.

It was no way to live.

• • •

I had no idea that the session with Deepak was just the beginning. That Oprah and her people were so moved by my story that they decided to have me be a guest. To go up on stage and share with the world that I was an alcoholic who had done the unimaginable one fateful day.

They were doing an Oprah's Lifeclass titled Growing Beyond Guilt. Boy, did I fit the bill. I sat on stage between Iyanla Vanzant and Oprah. Yep. On stage with Oprah. I couldn't really believe it was happening. And Iyanla's tough love and no bullshit approach truly changed my life.

To say that I wasn't nervous would be a lie. I was petrified to share my story with the world. I had already been experiencing the backlash and gossip that comes with living in a small town. It had been two years since the accident and enough time had gone by where I could leave my house to run an errand without being met with snide remarks or nasty looks as I walked through the grocery store or dropped one of my kids off at practice. People were starting to forget about the monster they perceived me to be and were into the next person's dirty laundry. The stones had stopped being thrown in my direction, and I wasn't sure that I was prepared, emotionally, to be in the line of fire again.

Gavin and Madison had already suffered tremendously as well from the backlash. The adults in my neighborhood still had very strong opinions about me and it showed in how their children teased and bullied Gavin and Madison. It was heartbreaking to watch them be ostracized and rejected by kids they thought were their friends and know that the parents were in full support. Many tears were cried by all of us on how hard it was to live among the whispers and passive taunts. The beer bottles thrown on our front lawn were just one of many reminders that we were not wanted.

The last thing I wanted was everything to start up again. The gossiping, the comments, the past were all simmering, and I wasn't about to throw another log on the fire and heat things up again.

The decision to do the show would mean that we were pulling off the Band-Aid on a still healing wound and I wasn't 100 percent convinced that I was ready. I was not made of steel.

It finally came down to this. Was I going to spend the rest of my life in a hole, too scared to face my critics and consequences or was I going to stand in my truth, with my husband and family by my side supporting me?

The hardest part was recounting the accident again. While the focus of the show was to help me move past my guilt, even Oprah said: "Well, I think that's something you should feel guilty about." I couldn't agree more. That was the exact reason I just couldn't seem to let go. I felt that I needed to feel guilty.

But then Iyanla began to talk. Iyanla knew what she was doing when she looked at me and said, "You've taken responsibility and are making different choices." It was so simple, so direct, so necessary. "Give yourself permission to be okay."

The tears began to course down my cheeks, I couldn't hold them back. "Stop telling that story," she continued, hitting every inch of my heart with her words. And she meant them.

In her stern and unsubtle way she woke me up. She gave me the willingness to set myself free. I no longer had to be chained to what I had done. It was over. I was giving myself permission to move forward and not allow my ego to steal my joy.

Oh, those words, they were just what I needed: to hear someone like her say I didn't need to feel guilty anymore, that I had learned the lesson, and that I had suffered enough.

It was the most freeing moment of my life.

©Harpo Studios, Inc., Photographer: George Burns

CHAPTER 32 *Matt*

I *gently placed Hadley in her crib* and turned on the monitor, brushing her soft hair off her forehead and giving her one final kiss. As I eased out the door, turning down the lights, I peeked into Madison and Gavin's rooms. Amy was curled up on Madison's bed with both kids tucked into her sides. I knew what they were doing. Not reading a bedtime story, but going over Amy's gratitude journal.

After rehab, Amy started journaling each night. Writing down the things she was thankful for: the moments of joy, the moments of significance, things that made her smile. She said it helped keep her out of her "poor me" I-hate-my-life trap. After a couple of months, it became a routine for her, and Madison started doing it, too. It was a sweet ritual, something that truly helped me transform my thinking about Amy. How could I hold a grudge when I saw how sweet she was being with our daughter, when she was teaching our children about the value of gratitude, saying thanks, whether it was to the people in your life or to God?

When no charges were brought, I felt like it was the universe saying that it was okay to move on. It was okay to forgive Amy. Ever since Hadley was born, I had slowly been rejoining our marriage and hoping that we might have a fresh start, but something about the miracle that she wasn't charged, even after the pleading I did, confirmed it for me. God was giving us a second chance.

But the real moment of clarity came when Amy started her master's program again. This was it: I had gotten my Amy back. She had always meant to get her master's in educational school counseling. After taking one class right about the time the Kelly stuff hit the fan, she quit. I was disappointed and always knew a program like that could focus her, could bring her back to me. But of course, it would take time and commitment, which at the time, she only had for alcohol.

As we began to see that charges might not come, her dad approached her. He had planned to cover her legal fees, but if that wasn't needed, he offered to pay for her master's program.

I saw Amy's face when he offered. It was a mix of pure joy, relief, and deep gratitude. She'd been talking about it for months, but we had no disposable income. It was hard to fathom taking our hard-earned money and putting it toward that when we still weren't covering our bills.

Plus, I knew she was so touched by this effort from her father. I knew their relationship had grown leaps and bounds since her stint in rehab. He was back in her life, had committed to getting sober as well, and was finally a father, not only to her, but also a grandfather to our children. To have his support in this way at this time in her life meant everything to Amy.

Our life was back on track. It was better than it had ever been before. I felt like I was a better person because of the person Amy was becoming. But in quiet moments, I could see Amy still struggling. I could see she still felt shackled to the guilt.

I tried to reason with her. One night after the kids were in bed, Amy was sitting at the kitchen table with a cup of tea, her journal in front of her. But her face looked haggard, her shoulders stooped. It looked like she was carrying the weight of the world.

I placed my hand on her shoulder, giving it a rub. She looked up at me with her eyes full of tears.

I pulled up a chair. "Babe," I said, "you have to forgive yourself. I forgive you. The kids forgive you. God forgives you. You have to stop punishing yourself."

She shook her head, her eyes squeezed shut as she tried to keep the tears from spilling out.

"I can't," she whispered.

I grabbed her hands, softly brushing my thumb across her knuckles, a gesture that tended to calm her. I even remembered doing it during all three labors with our kids.

"You got the lesson, babe," I said, trying to use some of the mantras she'd been focusing on in her spiritual journey. "We have faced the troubles in our marriage. You faced your alcoholism and are now two years sober. You've done it, Amy. Now you need to let go, and move forward."

She nodded. I knew she was trying. But the tentacles of shame were still trapped in her.

• • •

When Amy received another call from Oprah's team inviting her to appear on a show on guilt, I knew she was on the fence. Two years had passed since that fateful day and finally things were settling back to normal. We were still pretty unpopular in our community in many ways, but that had only driven us closer together. I put aside any friendships that couldn't support my decision to stay with her. That meant that finally it really was Matt and Amy against the world again.

But to go so public with our story? I knew it was risky. But honestly, if it kept her sober, I would do anything. Anything to keep her on this path. Anything for my bride.

One of the key phrases Amy kept repeating after rehab was "Healing, to me, means accepting responsibility." And I knew that I had my own responsibility in the mess we had made. I had come to realize that, in many ways, I was just as responsible for allowing the accident to happen. I was in my own pain, not able to respond to her cries for help. I was in denial and trying to "manage" everything by keeping an eye on her. As though I could control the outcome if I was there. But I wasn't always there. And toward the end, it was almost like I purposely wasn't there. Like I wanted her to fail so that I didn't have to deal with it anymore.

I have to live with that. Abandoning her when she needed my love the most.

I had to accept responsibility for how much I had given up on her. On us.

We went to three different marriage counselors during this time. All three didn't think we'd make it. I don't blame them, seeing the Mount Everest of issues we'd have to overcome. There were many times I couldn't see a way out of our mess either.

Most people still think that I am crazy for staying with Amy. For forgiving her. They don't know how I could move on, knowing what she did. It wasn't easy. My own family didn't talk to Amy for almost a year after the accident. Convincing them that she had changed while trying to stay committed myself was hard. We are all still rebuilding trust slowly, even now, after four years.

For me? I try to do my best to consider that that time period doesn't count. That wasn't my Amy. A demon had taken a hold of her. It had to be exorcised. And unfortunately, it took that accident to get it out.

When I think about all those years where she was such an embarrassment and out of control, I wonder why I didn't just pack my bags and head out.

All I can say is that I had the faith of a mustard seed. "I just knew you were in there," I tell her, every time she has doubts. And then I wrap her in a bear hug, so glad to have my bride back.

Obviously, we've had to do a lot of work to stay together. We've had to relearn how to be married. We have had to learn how to respond instead of react. How to let go and truly forgive in the moment instead of holding grudges and letting issues of the past fester and rot in the crevices of our love. We can't hang on to the past anymore. Not if we want our future.

And, of course, we've had to learn how to have fun without alcohol. That was a tough one for me. For a while, I was mad that I had to give up the social drinking so that Amy wouldn't be tempted. It was such a foundation of our social life. She'd changed the rules on me. But do I miss it enough to sacrifice my marriage? Hell no.

Today, those dark days seem so far behind us. Our family life has never been better. Amy inspires me to be a better person every day. My children now look at their mother with pride and respect, rather than uncertainty and shame. I look forward to seeing my wife each evening, rather than having a knot in my stomach from the unknown of what state she might be in. Our home is full of love, warmth, playfulness, and laughter rather than screaming, bitterness, and anger.

Amy and I got the lesson. And the lesson was: we have to learn to tell the truth. Period. Always. Whether it is easy or not.

The truth about what we want, what we need, and what we are willing to tolerate, both in our marriage and in life.

Is it hard to have this public accounting of our darkest days? Yes. But we wanted to share it, so that everyone could see that it is possible to move forward. We tell the story in both of our voices because we know, in every marriage, it's never just one person's fault. When you join together in front of God and your family, you become a team. I didn't understand what that meant until Amy showed me. It meant us having to take on each other's weaknesses, and support each other's strengths.

I know how close I was to giving up. Giving up on Amy and giving up on us. I couldn't be more thankful for the miracles that we were granted. Hadley's conception. The absence of charges. The new woman Amy has become. Every spiritual book she read, every time she let go a little bit more of the shame and guilt of the past, allowed us to step forward into our beautiful new life.

But none of that would have been possible if I had held on to my pride, and held back forgiveness. To forgive her was a gift to both Amy and myself. It granted us the power to move on.

It is absolutely amazing when I think about where our relationship once was and where it is now. When Amy was drinking, I didn't trust her, didn't believe a word she said, and really didn't want anything to do with her. I hated being around her. I hated seeing her get more and more out of shape. I hated that the kids had a mother they couldn't trust or believe. She would make them promises about things they were going to do on an upcoming weekend, but then would be too hungover to do them. I hated seeing the kids disappointed. Toward the end, I really couldn't help but imagine how much better things would soon be when I divorced her and moved on.

Today, it seems so long ago when we were in that position. I know it has only been four years of her being sober, but it seems like a lifetime. I couldn't be more proud of my wife. Although it took a tragedy to change things, Amy has become the best wife and mother of which a man and his children could ever dream. Her dedication and commitment to our family is nothing short of extraordinary.

It's almost funny to think about how I don't even question her when she tells me she has an errand to run. Back in her drinking days I would battle with her, take her car keys, follow her, simply because I knew what she was up to. Today, when she says she'll be home around a certain time, I believe her. I trust Amy 100 percent now. That is a great feeling to have in a marriage.

It's so refreshing to have our biggest arguments over whose turn it is to make the bed or whose job it was to pick up the dry cleaning. We laugh at our arguments now. Long gone are the arguments with bitter words, insults, and violence, most of which occurred in front of the kids.

I wish everyone in a marriage could experience the pure happiness that I enjoy in my marriage to Amy today. We have come so far. I just want others to know that there is no issue too big, no failure too great. Forgiveness is the most powerful tool in the world. I want to help others who are struggling with these same types of issues to experience what life could be like with proper help and guidance.

But I know I owe all of my happiness to my bride. Without her commitment and perseverance to her sobriety, our family's happiness would not be possible.

CHAPTER 33 *Amy*

I sat, *looking in the mirror*, pinning my graduation cap in place. I stared at the woman in the mirror, remembering that dark day when I didn't recognize the woman staring back.

Today, I recognized her. I was proud of her. Here I was, after all that had happened, about to receive my master's degree.

Three years ago I never would have believed it.

As I walked across the stage later that morning, the breeze blowing my hair, the sun beaming down, a sign of all the light and hope I felt within, I walked tall. Where once I was a girl curled in a corner afraid to face the world and drowning in my booze and burdens, I was now bold, happy, and self-assured. My children, husband, and family were seated in the audience, watching me end a chapter in my life and begin another.

· · ·

As I grew confident in my sobriety, Matt grew his confidence in me. As I began to trust my abilities, and myself, Matt, too, began to trust his decision and commitment to our union.

When Matt agreed to appear on the Oprah show with me, I knew that this was it. He was back in it, for good. There was no way he would appear on national television, spilling our dirty laundry, unless he was just as committed to my sobriety as I was. When I told him I wanted to go, to do it, I remember the look in his eyes.

"Okay, sounds good, I'll be there." He said, no hesitation, his eyes clear, encouraging, 100 percent behind me.

To feel that support, that unwavering support and belief in me was what I had been so desperate for all those years. I don't know why I did it, but I ran up to him and threw my arms around him.

"Thank you," I whispered into his neck.

It was a thank-you for doing the show, but it was for so much more. For not giving up. For giving me a chance. For forgiving me.

I could tell in his eyes. He didn't see me as a drunk, a screw-up anymore. He saw me as Amy. And yes, I had flaws. Yes, I would always have a weakness around alcohol. Yes, I might always have a temper on me, too. But he accepted me for all of it. And he loved me just the same.

Finally, we were in a place of peace, a place of forgiveness. Together we made the choice to move forward and not look back.

. . .

I had a conversation the other day with a friend of mine who continues to battle his addiction. It was hard to sit on the other end of the phone and listen to him try to justify his drinking and drugging. I found myself getting short and frustrated with him. He kept asking me the same questions over and over: "How did you do it?" or "What can I do?"

I gave him the answer. It just wasn't the answer he wanted to hear. So he would reword the question and ask, "What is the secret?" It was the same question, so I gave the same answer.

The problem with alcoholics is we want to complicate things. We aren't satisfied until we turn the simplest of things into a huge, full-fledged, blown way out of proportion kind of situation. That's the truth. For some reason we just can't see that the answer is so simple.

So, when my friend wasn't listening and accepting my answer, he reworded his question yet again. "How did you turn your life around?" I sighed. He still wasn't hearing me. The answer is as plain and as simple as the nose on our faces. The answer is . . . Stop drinking! How did I do it? I stopped drinking! What is the secret? I stopped drinking. How did I turn my life around? I stopped drinking.

Once we accept the truth about our problems, it's much easier to see the solution. I had a problem with alcohol and the solution was to stop drinking. It does not get much clearer than that. *Stop drinking* is all I kept repeating to him, but that is not what he wanted to hear. What he wanted me to say was that it was okay to drink because he had a rough childhood. He wanted me to condone his drinking because he had two failed marriages and was living day to day. What he wanted to hear me say was that I understood why he drank and that it was acceptable for him to continue to hit the self-destruct button because he was abused when he was younger, and alcohol gave him the outlet he needed to cope with those memories of his father. But I wouldn't give him that validation. I told him to stop drinking and to seek the guidance and the help of someone in recovery, because that is how he was going to survive the wreckage of his past and his future mistakes.

Living sober is not saying that you're never going to drink again. It *is* saying, however, that you're at least willing to try. And that is the place that we all have to be in when we decide to turn our will and our lives over to the care of God as we understand Him to be. Giving ourselves up to the universe or whatever is out there and willing to help us give sobriety a shot. We have to be willing, just for the day, the hour, the moment. We have to be willing to sacrifice booze for a better life. Is it easy? Hell no, but it's worth a shot, isn't it?

My transformation didn't happen overnight. It has taken time to learn to sit in the grace God has given me. But over time I began to realize that I was not living in his grace by condemning myself to life riddled with guilt. I wasn't embracing the second chance that God had given me.

I also had to learn to change my story. Instead of seeing myself as an alcoholic who almost killed her kids, I have to start with the fact that I am a redeemed woman, someone who knows that there is always light at the end of the tunnel no matter how dark it may seem.

So much of the battle is in my head. Quieting the inner voice reminding me of my past sometimes seems impossible. It takes constant diligence to not let those self-defeating, "poor me" thoughts seep back it. I used to replay the image of Madison on that stretcher in my mind and torture myself over it, until I learned how to stop the fixation I had on beating myself up. Only then was I able to regain control over my thoughts. I took a step back from my external world and went inward. I repeated over and over to myself, *My thoughts are not me, my thoughts are not me, my thoughts are not me.* I stopped telling myself, *You're a lousy mom, you're a drunk, you're no good.* Because I thought those things, I would feel those things. I had to stop saying out loud the hurtful and self-deprecating thoughts that were running through my mind all day long. I had to learn how to silence my inner voice that never shut up.

My new mantra has become, *I give myself permission to move forward, I give myself permission to be okay.*

There are still times when I think to myself that it's impossible and I feel discouraged. Matt and I still argue, I still think about a drink. Some days my life feels as though it's not getting any easier, and there are still those days when I feel like I can't move forward and I'm stuck. There are the occasional moments when I feel like giving up and grabbing a beer and fear that I will always be fighting a losing battle.

Those are the days when I need my program and my support system the most.

I don't know why I am able to stay sober and other people can't. I can't explain why some people find themselves back in rehab or jails over and over again. I wish I could answer those questions. I can only speak for myself and what worked for me. I choose to put my faith and trust in God. I choose to believe that there is something greater at work.

I began to pay attention to the messages my life was whispering to me. The intuitive feeling you get in the pit of your stomach or back of your mind telling you something isn't right or to get up and do something. I used to ignore those feelings until I learned that there was something greater at work going on around me. A force taking shape in my life that I couldn't see. You can call it whatever you want to but there still is no denying that it's there. When I was consumed by alcohol, I ignored the whispers of my life and listened only to the voice inside my head. I've had to change that.

To me, living sober is the best amends I have to offer anyone. As much as I want to, I can't change how I treated people while I was drinking or take back the words that came out of my mouth or alter the things I did while intoxicated. But I can choose not to drink today, and deciding not to drink every day is how I make my amends to my loved ones.

Life is tough. It will deliver blow after blow after blow. You can allow it to defeat you. You can turn to things that numb you and check you out. Maybe it's alcohol or drugs, maybe it's work or sex or food. Whatever it is that keeps you from feeling.

Or you can take what life has handed you and stand back up. Yes, you're bloody, bruised, and exhausted. But you are feeling it. You are there. You are present. And you know what? Deep down, you have the strength to face it.

Today, because I took the first step in admitting that I was powerless against my disease, I am able to hold my head high and believe that I am capable of change and deserving of a chance. I came to appreciate that only through utter defeat and humiliation was I able to start on the path to forgiveness and redemption. I have gained through my personal heartbreak an unshakable belief and conviction of the divine mercy of my God. I am in awe of the transformation my life has taken. Of how abundant my life can be without a drink. I have made the shift and am able to accept my faults along with my favors. But most important, I have learned what it means to live in His grace.

Go confidently in the directions of your dreams.
Live the life you've always imagined.

—Henry David Thoreau

Acknowledgments

We would like to express our gratitude to all those who saw us through this book; to those who provided support, love, honesty, and forgiveness along our journey.

Above all, we want to thank our parents, Joe and El, Ruth Ann and Larry, and Denny and Loretta, who supported and encouraged us in spite of our resistance for help and our faith. It was a long and difficult journey for them. We can't ever repay you for loving us so unconditionally or for having the strength and courage to lift us each time we fell. You stood tall behind us until we were able to walk alone.

We would like to thank HCI Books for giving us the opportunity to share our story. We give a special acknowledgment to Michele Martin and Steve Harris, our agents, who together helped to make our dream a reality.

We would like to express our great appreciation to Cindy DiTiberio for helping us with the process of telling our story and doing it so beautifully. We also thank Allison, our editor with HCI, who walked us through each step of publishing.

Thank you to Ms. Oprah Winfrey—without you, this book would never have found its way.

A very warm and special thank you to the OWN Ambassadors, you all have supported, uplifted, and inspired us every step of the way. We are truly blessed and fortunate to call each of you a friend.

To Margaret, without your love and devotion to my sobriety and friendship, none of this would be possible.

To Dr. David Rooney, thank you for having the patience and fortitude to see us through some of our darkest moments medically and personally.

Sue and Julie, thank you for never judging and your unwavering support. We are grateful.

To Carol, thank you for all those times you sat and listened.

To my work colleagues who gave so much of their time and compassion. Your generosity in providing comfort, meals, donations, and care to our children and us was appreciated and admired. The first weeks were the most difficult and your help gave us relief. We are most appreciative of the moments we've shared privately.

Thom, thank you for always being the big brother we needed you to be.

Last and not least, we thank God for blessing us far more than we probably deserve.

We ask forgiveness of all those who have been alongside us over the years and whose names we have failed to mention. We appreciate your love and hope that you continue to bless our lives with your friendship.

About the Authors

Amy **Baumgardner** is a freelance writer, mother, and wife. She was born in Pennsylvania and holds a master's degree in educational school counseling. Amy had the opportunity to share her story on an episode of Oprah's Lifeclass with Iyanla Vanzant on July 29, 2012, and is now an OWN Ambassador. Amy attributes her happiness to her faith and devoted husband. She has been sober for four years.

Matt **Baumgardner** was born in Clearfield, Pennsylvania, located in central Pennsylvania. He is the son of a public school teacher and registered nurse and is the oldest of three siblings. Matt attended Bloomsburg University, where he acquired a BS degree in elementary education. Later, he completed his master's degree at Wilmington University with a MEd in school leadership. Matt currently teaches middle-school American history in a southeastern Pennsylvania suburban school district.

Matt and Amy have three beautiful children, Gavin, twelve, Madison, ten, and Hadley, four. They live in Oxford, Pennsylvania. Visit their website at *www.mattandamyb.com*.

About the Writer

Cynthia DiTiberio has helped countless award-winning and *New York Times* bestselling authors of fiction and nonfiction take their writing to the next level. She worked as an editor at HarperOne Publishers for nine years before leaving the traditional publishing model to consult with writers directly. She is both an editor and collaborator and loves to help make ideas come to life on the page. She grew up in St. Louis, Missouri, graduated with a BA in religion from Wake Forest University, and now resides in Palo Alto, California, with her husband, daughter, and son. More information can be found at *www.cdteditorial.com*.

Book Club Questions

What is your reaction to the idea of forgiveness? Do you believe that everything is forgivable?

Everyone responds differently in matters of the heart. Instead of reacting in anger there can be a quiet, subtle reaction to a broken heart and hurt feelings. How do you respond to those who hurt you? Do you react in anger, fear, love, or judgment? Do you feel cynical toward the whole idea of forgiveness as a requirement to moving forward?

Why do you think people are content to hold on to the past when the release of forgiveness is available?

Do you agree with how Matt reacted to Amy's drinking?

Think of the person who has caused you the most pain . . . now imagine forgiving that person. What would that feel like for you to be able to release those resentments?

At what point did you see Matt begin to forgive Amy? At what point did you see Amy start to forgive herself?

Do you believe that Matt and Amy's faith played a role in their ability to forgive? Why or why not?